'In this must-read book, Shlomo Ben-Hur launches a broad-based call to action to the learning function and to senior line management. Learning at the speed of change has become a question of survival. As both a practitioner, who was a co-creator of the CLIP accreditation process for corporate universities, and a leading academic, Shlomo has a unique profile from which he derives the authority to show ways out of the crisis in corporate learning.'

Richard Straub,
Director of Corporate Services,
European Foundation for Management Development (EFMD)

'Drawing on his experience as former Vice President of Leadership Development and Learning for the BP Group, as well as on his close work at IMD with Fortune 500 companies, Professor Ben-Hur suggests seven key activities to help your company transform corporate learning into stronger business results. It is a must-read for all learning professionals, as well as business leaders who are interested in turning learning into a sustainable competitive advantage.'

Dominique Turpin,
President, IMD

'Most corporations have recognised the central role that learning can play in their success, but neither the market nor researchers offer clear guidance on how best to proceed. Shlomo Ben-Hur's book provides a welcome alternative to what's available in the learning space. He clarifies the central role of learning, articulates the central decisions that leaders must make, and lays out possible pathways to success. The book rests on solid research foundations, but it applies them to business cases in ways that will be useful to practitioners and informative for researchers.'

Stanton E.F. Wortham,
Judy & Howard Berkowitz Professor and Associate Dean, Penn GSE;
Academic Director, Penn Chief Learning Officer Doctoral Program

The Business of Corporate Learning

Insights from Practice

SHLOMO BEN-HUR
IMD, Switzerland

CAMBRIDGE
UNIVERSITY PRESS

University Printing House, Cambridge CB2 8BS, United Kingdom

One Liberty Plaza, 20th Floor, New York, NY 10006, USA

477 Williamstown Road, Port Melbourne, VIC 3207, Australia

314-321, 3rd Floor, Plot 3, Splendor Forum, Jasola District Centre, New Delhi - 110025, India

79 Anson Road, #06-04/06, Singapore 079906

Cambridge University Press is part of the University of Cambridge.

It furthers the University's mission by disseminating knowledge in the pursuit of
education, learning and research at the highest international levels of excellence.

www.cambridge.org
Information on this title: www.cambridge.org/9781107027008

First published 2013
5th printing 2014

A catalogue record for this publication is available from the British Library

Library of Congress Cataloging in Publication data
Ben-Hur, Shlomo, 1962–
    The business of corporate learning : insights from practice / Shlomo Ben-Hur.
        pages   cm
    Includes bibliographical references and index.
    ISBN 978-1-107-02700-8
    1. Organizational learning.   2. Corporations.   I. Title.
    HD58.82.B457 2013
    658.3'124–dc23
    2012038089

ISBN 978-1-107-02700-8 Hardback

DEDICATION

To my parents, Moshe and Clair, who instilled in me a true passion for learning which continues to be a guiding force in my life.

And to my treasured family, who fill my learning journey with inspiration and love: my wife Robin and our children Daniel and Arielle.

Contents

Figures

Tables

Acknowledgements

The seeds of this book began germinating during my corporate career, as I was enchanted by my successes and humbled by my failures in trying to help organisations to learn. However, it was only after I joined the faculty of IMD business school in Switzerland that I started believing in the value of sharing these lessons with IMD's corporate partners, many of whom are wrestling with similar dilemmas. Through IMD's Corporate Learning Discovery Events and the Chief Learning Officer Roundtable, which I chair, I have had the distinct privilege of not only sharing my insights but also clarifying my thinking and furthering my understanding of the issues in this book.

To fully acknowledge all of those who have contributed to this book by shaping my experience, I would have to write a detailed autobiography, which is not possible here. However, I would like to mention a number of people without whom this book would not have come to life.

I am deeply grateful to my colleague Gordon Shenton, whose thoughtful ideas and wisdom are behind Chapter 2 of this book. I met Gordon eight years ago at the European Foundation for Management Development in Brussels. He brought a group of chief learning officers from a number of European multinational corporations together there to develop the CLIP accreditation scheme for corporate universities, which has since become an established quality label on the global corporate learning scene. Gordon and I have spent many days over the last two years discussing this book and its various chapters, and I will always be indebted to him for his inspiration, illumination and encouragement of my nascent ideas.

In chronological order of my corporate learning journey, I thank my former DaimlerChrysler Services Academy team and my BP Learning and Leadership Development team. It was an honour to manage these two global teams of learning professionals, in which each and every member of the teams enlivened my continuing journey along the road towards a deeper understanding of the complexities of corporate learning.

Most significantly, my appreciation of my colleague and friend Nik Kinley is immeasurable. I originally met Nik on the BP team, and he has supported my work on this book in inestimable ways, including critically reading and editing the manuscript, challenging my thinking, and forcing me to solidify my opinions. I could not have written this book without him.

On the IMD side, I would like to thank IMD's president Dominique Turpin and my deans Robert Hooijberg and Anand Narasimhan for their support and encouragement of my research and writing. I thank Joe DiStefano and Dan Denison for supporting my life transition from the corporate sector to a full-time academic career, and I am grateful to John Weeks for helping me break into my new vocation. Special thanks go to Persita Egeli and Cédric Vaucher, for guiding me through the world of research publishing, and to the entire research and editing teams for their ongoing support of my multiple projects. I am especially indebted to Lindsay McTeague for her outstanding support during the last month of this journey in editing the chapters and creating the final manuscript.

For keeping me inspired along this path and believing in the power of organisational learning, I would like to thank the valued corporate contributors who are behind the cases mentioned in the book: Urbain Bruyere of BP, Steven Smith of Capgemini, Clare O'Brien of Disney/ABC Television Group, Andrew Kilshaw of Nike and Frank Waltman of Novartis.

I would also like to thank my Cambridge University Press editor Paula Parish, whose editorial guidance helped make this book more targeted and bring this project to completion.

And finally, to my parents Moshe and Clair, who instilled in me a true passion for learning which I brought to my work of building both individual abilities and organisational capabilities. And, most wholeheartedly, I want to express my deepest love to my wife and partner Robin and my children Daniel and Arielle, who have travelled with me on this journey of self-discovery and in my career in the field of learning. I continue to learn from each of you every day.

1 The weight of history: an introduction

The traditional way to begin a story or book, at least in many European languages, is with the phrase 'once upon a time'. As starts go, it's not a bad one. Yet in thinking about the first words of this book, it occurred to me that I couldn't begin this way, as this opening is usually paired with the equally traditional ending of '... and they all lived happily ever after'. And quite frankly, I am not sure that corporate learning will.

This book, then, is about corporate learning and about what organisations need to do to make it work. Like so many stories, it is a tale of desire and frustration, of good intentions and misplaced actions. Whether it will be a tragedy or just a drama remains to be seen, but it begins with a crisis and, indeed, it is this crisis that makes me fervently believe that this tale needs telling.

In 2004 a well-publicised survey found that only 17 per cent of business leaders reported being 'very satisfied' with the performance of their learning functions.[1] In the intervening period, there has been no shortage of books, articles and opinions about how to rectify the situation. Yet nothing much seems to have changed because in early 2012 another survey found that more than half of line managers believe that employee performance would not change if the company's learning function were eliminated. That is pretty damning. It would be nice if we could dismiss this as 'just one survey', but the reality is that over the past ten years research has repeatedly shown that the proportion of business leaders who report being satisfied with their learning function's performance has steadfastly remained around 20 per cent.[2]

In my work with some of the world's top learning and business leaders, I see this dissatisfaction on a daily basis. And I see its impact in the frustrations of learning leaders that their budgets are always the first to be cut, that they are struggling for their function to be seen as a strategic one, and that their department is continually being restructured and repositioned in the organisation. This scenario is cause for concern in its own right, but it gets worse. Fuelled by downturn-driven budgetary pressures and apprehension about the efficacy of learning interventions, demand for evidence of the impact and value of learning is growing fast.[3] In fact, demonstrating the value of learning is *the* number one challenge reported by learning executives today.[4] So a lack of progress in improving and proving the impact of learning is suddenly meeting both heightened and hardened expectations. Something needs to change and it needs to change fast, because the stark reality is that for the past decade we appear as a profession generally to have been coming up short, and with attention on us like never before, it looks as if we will not be able to continue doing so for much longer without losing what remains of our credibility.

So I was compelled to write this book by worry and concern. And what worries me most is not so much the obvious poor standing of corporate learning as a profession, but two other related issues. The first is the apparent lack of progress in improving our standing, despite significant amounts of effort and activity. There is little doubt that the past ten years have witnessed big changes in the practice of corporate learning, that things are and have been developing. Indeed, the journals are full of case studies of genuinely fascinating, innovative and apparently excellent practice. But what intrigues and really worries me is that the apparent lack of progress comes in spite of all this activity. It is not that things have not been happening or changing, it is that any changes have either not been the right ones or have not been enough. Not only do we need to change something, but whatever we do must also be different from and better than what we've tried up to now.

The second cause of my worry relates to the finding that today's learning leaders persistently report their top challenge to be demonstrating the value of their work. I share their concern on this point: demonstrating value *is* a challenge and one that we will look at later in the book. But I am surprised that it comes out as *the* number one concern. My fear is that this finding reveals an assumption that lurks in the background of our profession – the idea that there is nothing wrong with what we are doing at present, that we are already adding value, and that the consistently miserable satisfaction ratings from business leaders are somehow not a fair reflection of what we do. It is as if the issues we face are skin-deep, challenges of presentation and political positioning more than the substance of our work.

I could not disagree more. I am certain that the learning profession can, and often does, add value. I have seen and been involved in pieces of work that have made a difference to organisations. Yet I also believe that our poor standing as a profession is not just about presentation. The stark, harsh and painful reality is that something we are doing is not working. Top to toe, something is wrong and it is going to take more than a change in how we present and position ourselves to put things right.

So we have a crisis, and a big one at that. But it is not all doom and gloom. This book is born of hope, too, because as skill shortages and decreasing opportunities to achieve competitive advantage drive businesses to look internally, learning leaders have the attention of their organisations like never before. We may be under greater pressure to deliver, but we also have the stage and the opportunity to put things right. Indeed, there is already a seismic shift occurring, as the corporate learning function strives to move from being a responsive service function to an agenda-setting, value-producing enterprise.[5] Whether it will succeed remains to be seen.

In this book I lay out what I believe needs to happen for the corporate learning function to successfully make this transition and gain a seat at the strategic table. It is an accumulation of my experience of delivering learning, my observations of others doing so, and the many dialogues I have conducted with learning professionals around the world. It is my answers to the questions of what the learning function should change now, how exactly it can go about doing so, and – critically – why the changes in the profession over the past decade have not produced any lasting, visible improvement. I begin by addressing this last question and look at an example of a Big Idea that captured people's imaginations, was widely seen as capable of fundamentally transforming the field of corporate learning and yet, ultimately, failed to do so.

A BIG BANG WITH LITTLE IMPACT

The years immediately after the Second World War may have been hard economically, but they were boom times for theorists and researchers. One of the ideas that emerged just before the war was systems theory, which had the grand aim of trying to identify general rules that could explain the behaviour of all the different types of systems in every field of science. After the war, one of the outgrowths of this thinking was the field of cybernetics: the study of how things (both mechanical and biological) process information, react to information and change because of it. Inspired by these ideas, people began applying them to organisations during the 1950s and 1960s with the goal of trying to help organisations work more effectively as systems.

One of the leading lights in this movement was Donald Schön. His highly influential book, *Beyond the Stable State*, published in 1973, popularised the idea that the modern world is constantly changing and that if systems are to be effective they have to be flexible and able to adapt to meet the ever-changing demands of this environment. In Schön's view, *organisational learning* was the key process that enabled this flexibility and adaptation; for businesses to be successful, they needed to be able to learn.

Over the course of the next decade, Schön, in partnership with Chris Argyris, went on to explore how organisational learning could be made to happen. Yet the person who really took this on and whose name is perhaps most associated with the idea, is

Peter Senge. In 1990 Senge published his seminal book *The Fifth Discipline: The Art and Practice of the Learning Organisation.* In it, he proposed five conditions for learning: an understanding of the ways people interpret events and structure their thinking; the possibility of effective team learning; the capacity to build a shared vision of where the organisation wants to go; the personal mastery of individuals within the organisation in growing their self-awareness and ability to develop; and the ability to see issues holistically, to think systemically and to understand the connections between all the parts of a system. Senge argued that effective organisational learning only happens when these five conditions all occur together, resulting in what he called *generative learning*: learning that enables organisations not only to adapt to their environment but also to change and innovate in proactive anticipation of it.

The Big Idea that Schön, Argyris and Senge envisaged together was an ideal state – the *learning organisation* – that they believed all businesses should strive towards. It was a state in which organisations continuously learnt and purposefully transformed themselves and in which learning was *the* key competency required for sustaining competitive advantage.

It is important to understand how radical these ideas were. From a traditional viewpoint, learning was planned and delivered through formal programmes, with the objective of achieving predefined outcomes, such as the acquisition of a specific skill or piece of knowledge. In the new worldview, though, learning was a spontaneous, ongoing process that was embedded in unplanned everyday activities; its objective was to promote the process of learning itself, rather than specific intended outcomes. It was a heady idea, seeming to promise an entirely new approach not only to learning but also – with its emphasis on open, democratic collaboration – to the entire social structure of the business. Schön and Senge saw themselves as pragmatic idealists and always positioned themselves as practitioners rather than theorists, but there was nonetheless a crusading belief in the possibility they raised of a transformed corporate world.

In the early 1990s, being a learning organisation became the desired status throughout the corporate United States. Like ripples on a pond, the concepts of the new worldview spread out, generating further discussion and ideas as they went. Much of this discussion was pragmatic, for instance on how exactly to integrate the learning occurring in individuals into some kind of broader pattern of knowledge of value to the organisation. One step in this direction was the rise of knowledge management in the early 1990s. A barely used phrase before this time, it became commonplace in the latter part of the decade as organisations began to focus on how knowledge was created, retained and disseminated, in an effort to ensure organisational learning occurred and to boost intellectual capital and innovation. Some companies even went as far as creating a knowledge management function within their corporate HR or Group Strategy department.

And yet, despite all the advantages, the revolution faltered and the era of the learning organisation failed to appear. There was, for sure, no shortage of case studies of organisations achieving elements of the ideal, but overall, corporate learning as a discipline failed to change, or at least it did not change enough. For all the promise of the ideas, their practical application within organisations was limited. This is not to say that they had no impact at all. Many of the ideas from this period underpin the way we currently understand and approach corporate learning. There is still widespread agreement that learning can be one of the keys to corporate survival and success and to maintaining competitive advantage. The distinctions between individual learning and organisational learning remain as crucial as ever, as does the core challenge of finding ways to link the two. And the importance of a systemic approach has likewise remained, as evidenced by the increased interweaving of learning with culture change initiatives.

But the promise and compelling excitement of the learning organisation ultimately failed to transform the business of learning. The reasons for this failure are our main interest here, and there were three main ones. First, the concepts of the learning organisation by and large failed to materialise into actual operational systems, processes and practices: there was a lack of easily implementable mechanisms to bring it to life. It is an irony that an approach that set so much store by systems thinking failed to embody itself in the structures and systems of the corporate world, and thus remained a floating, disembodied ideal. Second, the approach was so resolutely focused on driving learning processes, rather than outcomes, that it was difficult to clearly link its objectives to organisations' priorities and strategic agendas. At a time when a focus on short-term results, cost-cutting and restructuring was all the rage, this was a fatal flaw.

Finally, while the logic of the learning organisation was pointing in one direction, the reality of the political and economic environments was leading in another. With the end of the Cold War and the relaxing of global trade barriers, globalisation became a dominant factor in corporate life and thus corporate learning. Corporate universities emerged in companies around the globe and the focus shifted to coordinating and standardising. While these trends were not in themselves inherently oppositional to the ideals of the learning organisation, they led to the emergence of central coordinating learning units whose activities were very different to these ideals. These new units were integrated into businesses' operating processes, had close links to executive decision-making bodies and, in the best cases, existed explicitly to support the strategic priorities of the organisation. It marked the rise of the modern corporate learning function, a far cry from the ideal of the learning organisation.

Although there was nothing inherently wrong with the ideals of the learning organisation, they did not make sense in the environment in which they existed and they were not sufficiently grounded to help learning leaders understand what to do to take them forward. I believe that their day may still come, but it is not today because many of the same challenges persist.

TWO LESSONS FROM HISTORY

The lesson we can learn from this exemplar of promise and failure is that the change corporate learning needs to make, the solution it needs to find to its current woes, has to be viable in the current corporate context. For a change to make a difference, it must first fit in.

So what environment does it need to fit in with? There is of course no single common global environment, but certain trends do stand out. For starters, we work with a hard focus on outcomes, with metrics being used more than ever before to guide organisations' decision-making. We face growing talent strain, with demand for talent increasing and supply decreasing. By 2020, India will be the only net exporter of talent in the world. Phrases such as 'talent intelligence' and 'talent analytics' are becoming popular, as businesses redouble their efforts to find, grow and accelerate the development of the capability of their people. Leaner, matrixed organisations are increasingly the norm and as organisations continue to be de-layered, it is the middle that is squeezed, with managers reporting higher levels of stress and less time to manage their people. Product life cycles are growing shorter. 'Strategic alignment' is a phrase seemingly never far from people's lips. Technology is changing how we work and learn. And we are changing, too: generational shifts in how we work and what we expect from work are being heralded and may even materialise.

This is the world we live in. This is the world in which changes we make to improve the impact of corporate learning have to make sense and add value. So our solutions to the crisis facing corporate learning should speak not only to the issues and challenges in the way corporate learning goes about its work but also to the external challenges that businesses are facing. The bar is high, and reaching it will not be easy because we – like the proponents of the learning organisation – begin with one foot stuck firmly to the floor. For corporate learning, like all things, is laden with history, with hidden assumptions, ideas and concepts that originate from bygone days and may or may not fit our times. These historical assumptions and traditions impact both how others see corporate learning and how corporate learning sees itself: what it understands its role to be, and the ways in which it seeks to fulfil this role.

Take, for example, the very word 'learning'. It conjures up a traditional, academic view that tends to involve talking and thinking about learning as either the accumulation of knowledge or the acquisition of skills. This sounds reasonable enough. Yet the element that provides value to organisations – the *application* of the knowledge or the skill – is missing. As I explain later in the book, I believe that in this sense corporate learning is not and should not be about learning at all; rather it is about behaviour change and performance improvement. This does not mean that the acquisition of skills and knowledge is not important but that, ultimately, this is not the goal of corporate learning, not what it is about.

So we are weighed down by history, betrayed by the very language we use to describe what we are trying to do. The challenge that corporate learning faces in solving its current crisis is not merely to produce an environmentally sensitive and embedded solution that makes sense in its time. It is not just to produce something practical and easily implementable. The challenge is also to develop an understanding of the way in which our history channels our thinking and renders us prone to certain biases, so that we can adopt a fresher, more objective perspective. To move forward, we need to escape the weight of history.

ABOUT THIS BOOK

These, then, are the criteria that we as learning professionals must use to test the solutions I propose in this book: our litmus test for success. They must be environmentally sensitive, easily implementable and as free from historical bias as possible. In the remaining chapters, I cover the seven key activities that comprise corporate learning. I explore the challenges involved, explain how practice has – or has not – changed over the years, and make clear recommendations about how corporate learning needs to adapt to deal with the crisis it faces. Chapter 2 focuses on strategically aligning corporate learning, on how to construct a strategically focused, centrally positioned corporate learning function that is capable of adding real value to the organisation. Chapter 3 looks at how we develop corporate learning solutions, and Chapter 4 explores how they can best be delivered, looking in particular at the impact of the changing technological environment on what we do. Chapter 5 focuses on resourcing the corporate learning function, on how the roles of learning professionals are changing and need to change further, and on the options available to organisations for resourcing learning, including outsourcing. Chapter 6 addresses how to demonstrate and report the value of corporate learning, tackling the thorny and persistently problematic issue of evaluation. Chapter 7 looks at the branding and positioning of corporate learning, and Chapter 8 focuses on governance and what we have to do to make sure that, once back on track, we stay there. The book concludes, in Chapter 9, by proposing a way forward.

Going through these seven components, I show how and why corporate learning needs to change in *all* of them. And make no bones about it, to achieve the transformation required will be an incredibly difficult task. Many of the proposed changes are small evolutions, yet taken together they amount to nothing short of a revolution. The aim is to create a tipping point, a point at which corporate learning will be fundamentally altered and able as a result to improve its standing and achieve the seat it desires, and should have, at the corporate strategic table.

Although I have some strong views on particular things that need to change and how they should change, for the most part I do not present a detailed, prescriptive account of exactly what learning leaders ought to do, but rather provide a map of the key decision points they will face. I have chosen to focus on decision points because, although there are some rules of thumb, there is no single right way of doing things. The world is too complex and ever-changing. The last thing learning leaders need is another set of generic 'answers' – a guide on how to proceed will stand them in better stead. In fact, one of the most common things I hear in my work with learning leaders is, 'Where do I start?'

Consider the following real-life example of the scenario facing a learning leader when she joined a complex multinational organisation as its new chief learning officer (CLO). One of the first things she did was to map out the learning landscape (see Figure 1.1).

Faced with this 'ball of spaghetti', no wonder the leader was horrified by what she found. Untangling the mess, she knew, would be no easy thing. And of course the challenges of the structural disentanglement required were exacerbated by both a fragmented technological infrastructure and the political issues involved: the web of competing and often conflicting viewpoints about what corporate learning should be, what it should do and who should do it. Indeed, in this particular example, the learning leader ultimately failed in her attempts, undermined by a basic lack of executive agreement as to the mission and mandate of the learning function.

So the task ahead is complex, as amply evidenced not only by this example but also by our general failure to make progress over the past decade. Yet we do need to find a way forward. Without wanting to sound too dramatic, the future of corporate learning depends upon it. For too long, we have lived in a protective bubble, which has allowed us to continue to operate despite our generally miserable approval ratings, albeit with the occasional restructuring and budget cut when times got hard. Yet all the signs are that the honeymoon is well and truly over, as demonstrated by the growth in learning outsourcing. If we cannot produce what businesses want, they will find someone who can, or at least another provider who will tell them it can.

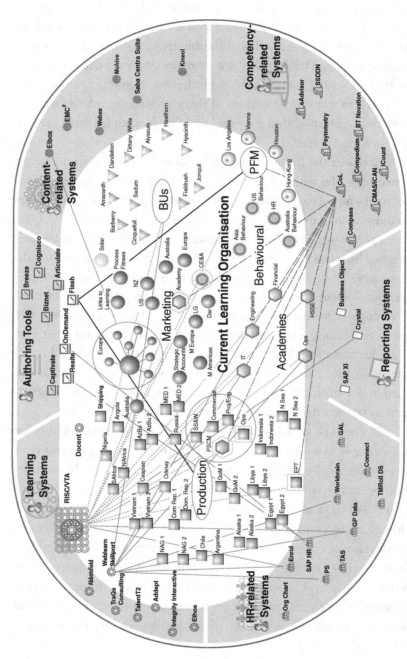

FIGURE 1.1 The learning landscape of a multinational corporation

If we fail, if we cannot make learning work, then we risk not only losing our jobs but also corporate learning as an endeavour drifting into the realm of irrelevance and becoming a tick-box activity tolerated by organisations because they feel they ought to be doing it, rather than because they really believe it can add value. Indeed, how many businesses are there where this is already the case? While business leaders may not be satisfied with what we as a profession tend to produce, for the most part they still appear to be convinced by the link between learning spend and organisational performance.[6] They are still believers in the theory, even if they feel the practice has been letting them down. We must act while they still are.

2 Creating a corporate learning strategy: how to align components to create coherence and impact

In the 1975 blockbuster movie *Jaws*, when the actor Roy Scheider sees the sheer size of the shark they have gone to hunt, he mutters, 'We're going to need a bigger boat.' These days the phrase is used when a situation seems insurmountable. I don't know what the chief learning officer mentioned in Chapter 1 said to herself when she first saw the spaghetti ball diagram of the learning structure she had inherited, but in my imagined reconstruction it was Scheider's line. Or at least, it should have been.

Not all spaghetti balls are as large or as complex, of course, but most corporate learning functions will have their version of one: their own structural, political and financial entanglements that they need to unwind. This chapter is about how to do that unwinding, and about how to create clarity and simplicity no matter how complex the environment. It is about how to develop a tool capable of cutting through such complexity. It is about how to build a bigger boat.

The basic tool you, as a learning professional, require is a strategic plan. Whether you are building, rebuilding or simply extending a learning function, you are going to need a strategy, and a good one at that. When asked, as I sometimes am, what makes for a good learning strategy, I tend to reply, 'alignment, alignment, alignment'. The first thing that springs to mind for most people when they hear this is the importance of aligning learning strategy with organisational strategy. That is hardly surprising, if you consider the volume of academic papers, magazine articles and blogs all articulating this core theme: that if learning is to be relevant for businesses, if it is to be perceived as valuable, then it has to be aligned to their objectives.

The weight of this opinion may sometimes have been slow to translate into practice, but it has nonetheless become a fundamental principle that few would argue with.

Yet when I talk of 'the importance of alignment', this is not usually what I mean. Let's be clear: I do ardently advocate the importance of aligning your corporate learning strategy with business objectives. But taking this as a given, I have become more interested in the *how* of it: how learning leaders can align the various components of their strategy with this principle and – critically – how they can align the components with one another, to create a coherent, focused and impactful corporate learning strategy. Because, at the risk of sounding heretical, I believe that aligning your learning function's structures and processes behind a clear, mandated learning strategy is as important as aligning your learning strategy with business objectives, if not more so. Yes, if your strategy is not aligned with the business, the chances are that what you do will not be perceived as valuable, but if you don't align your function behind your strategy, or if your strategy is not clear and mandated, you will not be able to do much at all.

MAPPING OUT A LEARNING STRATEGY

In the following pages, I lay out a map for how to build a learning strategy and align your function behind it. The map highlights five key issues that need to be addressed, each of which is a critical decision area, with choices to be made and challenges to be navigated (see Figure 2.1). My purpose in presenting this map is not to lay down a single 'right way' of doing things, but rather to reveal some of the 'right questions' that should be asked and answered. Moreover, I realise it would be possible to write a whole book (or two) on formulating a strategy, so my aim here is to underscore some of the key issues.

In visualising this map, there are three activities running vertically, from establishing a mandated mission, through defining its scope, to the positioning of the learning function within the company. Either side, there are the operational model of the function and

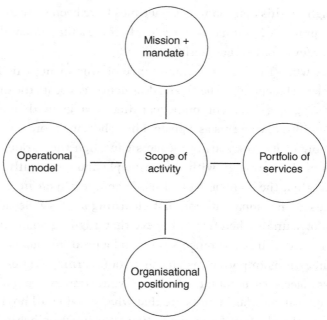

FIGURE 2.1 The strategically aligned learning function

constructing a portfolio of services, which together help ensure the system works effectively.

Mandating the mission

The starting point in our decision pathway is the core purpose of the corporate learning function: its mission and its mandate. By 'mission' we mean purpose, and by 'mandate' we mean the level of support that this purpose enjoys. Traditionally, or at least since the 1980s, an organisation's or function's purpose has been articulated in a 'mission statement'. These statements have a pretty bad reputation in many quarters, regarded as pointless exercises that are shoved in a drawer once they have been drafted, never to be looked at again. And it has to be said that I have seen my fair share of mission statements that do indeed appear pointless and are never used. But that is not because there is something wrong with mission statements per se, it is just that they have been poorly executed.

Unfortunately the bad reputation of mission statements has led some learning leaders to skip them, especially in hard-nosed business environments that view such statements as 'fluffy' and a waste of time. In fact, when I recently asked a group of learning teams gathered at IMD business school in Lausanne, Switzerland, whether they had a well-formulated mission and a clear mandate, a surprisingly large proportion – nearly half – replied that they did not. My main message, which I cannot overemphasise, is that mission statements – or whatever you choose to call them or disguise them as – are absolutely essential to the success of any learning function.

It is sometimes argued that drafting a mission statement is an endeavour that misses the essential point. What really counts, this argument goes, is the strength of conviction and sense of purpose among the members of the learning function and those that support it in the company's executive team. It is certainly true that no written statement by itself will ever replace an emotional sense of purpose, and that without buy-in any statement is not going to accomplish much. But this does not negate the need for having a statement and the benefits of having a good one.

Mission statements – done well – express the rationale behind the learning function's existence, the answers to some of the most fundamental questions. What is the function expected to achieve? What is its role within the company? Why, in other words, does it exist? Being able to provide convincing, well-articulated answers to these questions is important, and not just to avoid looking silly. If you do not have an agreed purpose, then you cannot have an explicit mandate to operate; and if you do not have a mandate, then you are operating on borrowed time, as the CLO with the spaghetti ball found out to her cost. This may sound obvious and straightforward, but in my experience creating a mandated mission statement is rarely straightforward. Indeed, if it feels easy, you are probably not doing it right.

Identifying the mission
The reason creating a mission statement can be difficult is that it requires agreement on three things: the core purpose of the learning

function; the key goals required to fulfil this purpose; and how best to put it all into words. The end objective is the two or three short statements that are readily understandable, credible and capable of generating buy-in across the company. Anyone reading them should immediately understand both your purpose in the organisation and the key missions you are focused on achieving.

Of course, answering questions such as 'Why do we exist?' is not easy. Generations of philosophers are testament to that. So where do you start? A popular place to begin is with the initial decision to create a central learning function. The founding purpose is itself not always clear, and in some cases the fact that it *is* clear may be unfortunate. I have seen businesses, for example, where the motivation for founding the function is rooted primarily in a 'me too' desire to follow the trend. Thus although the founding purpose may be a good place to start, in my experience it is sometimes not the best place to finish. Indeed, my general rule here is that although it is important to consider why the function has existed to date, what is most critical for the mission statement is to reflect why it should continue to exist.

There are instances where the core purpose may or should remain partly unstated. For example, some corporate learning functions that are narrowly focused on senior executive levels may serve primarily as a forum for the CEO and board members to pass down strategic messages to the top layers of management. This may be best left unsaid. Similarly, whenever a corporate learning function is created at a central level on top of pre-existing regional or divisional learning teams, the emphasis in communications is almost always on the strategic dimension – on the fact that the new central team will have business-wide objectives that cut across divisional and geographical lines. Yet another, less articulated, purpose is often also present, namely the desire to coordinate, harmonise and rationalise. Indeed, developing a mission statement is often as much about choosing what not to say as choosing what to say.

The need to involve key stakeholders in crafting the document can make the process all the more difficult, but it is also the source of much of the value to be gained from mission statements. It is likely to bring together people who may have opposing ideas about the learning function's core purpose, and the role of the learning leader is to try to knit these different ideas together. To return to the CLO with the spaghetti ball in Chapter 1, this was her key challenge: the head of HR (to whom she reported) and some of the business's key division heads had very different visions for the learning function, and the CEO was unwilling to step in to resolve the matter. Ultimately, no agreement emerged so the CLO was left both without a clear object-ive and with no real authority to deliver. This latter issue is at the heart of it. Without clear buy-in from key stakeholders as to the core purpose and main mission of the learning function, it effectively has no authority to act. Having a clear mission is not enough: the busi-ness has to agree that it is the right one.

Wording the mission

Once you have identified these things, finding the right words to articulate them is also often harder than expected. You need to choose terms that are sufficiently inspiring without falling into the trap of overdoing it and making statements that sound exaggerated or not credible. There is also a temptation to use buzzwords that have become trivialised through overuse, such as *empowering*, *ener-gising* and *maximising*. Glossy presentation must not become a sub-stitute for real substance.

It is also important to be precise. Failure to be sufficiently spe-cific in defining the mission makes it hard for the learning func-tion to plan its range of target audiences and areas of intervention. Moreover, the more clearly the outcomes are defined, the easier it is to determine whether or not the objectives have been met. Or to put it another way, a loosely drafted mission statement makes it difficult to prove that you have succeeded in it.

Finally, it is also worth thinking about the emphasis placed on reactivity or proactivity. In most mission statements the focus is squarely on the first of these, reflected in phrases such as 'responsive to business needs'. The learning function is thus charged with reactive tasks that are effectively assigned to it, such as implementing competency frameworks and cascading new product training. All corporate learning functions should be reactive in this way to some extent. Yet in order to contribute to strategy review and formation, the learning function has to be proactive as well. Proactive statements give the learning function a role in generating new ideas, searching for better ways of doing things, or helping the company learn about its environment, markets and customers. These issues are particularly pertinent when the business proclaims that it sees itself as a 'learning organisation' that encompasses creativity, critical thinking and an enquiring mindset. Ideally, the mission statements of all learning functions will encompass both reactive and proactive goals.

With a clear, well-worded and agreed mission statement, you have a compass bearing to guide you. You have a reference point you can return to whenever the course ahead is unclear, a checkpoint for all the decision points you encounter as you seek to disentangle complexities. You also increase the likelihood that members of the learning function will work with a strong sense of purpose and that stakeholders will understand the learning function's role in the company. The strength of the function, its perceived legitimacy and its ability to survive the ups and downs of corporate life will obviously depend on the efficacy of its work, the quality of its systems and the credibility of its staff, but mission statements are a glue that binds these elements together and ensures they are aligned.

Assessing the corporate learning mission

Questions to ask yourself when developing a mission statement

1. Is your core purpose clear?
2. Has your corporate learning function's mission been formulated effectively? Do you have an explicit mission statement?
3. Does it specify what the corporate learning function is expected to achieve?
4. Does the mission have the full support of the learning function staff, senior business executives and frontline management?

5. Is the mission understood by people throughout the company?
6. Does the mission statement include any jargon that could be perceived negatively?
7. Is the mission compatible with the cultural reality and business traditions of the company?
8. Is the mission realistic in view of the environmental constraints under which the company operates?
9. Does the corporate learning function have a clear mandate to act that is agreed by all key stakeholders?
10. Is the mandate backed up by sufficient authority to act?
11. Is there a process in place to enable the mission to be reviewed and updated in line with changing priorities?

Defining your scope

So you have a mission and a mandate, authority of purpose. But how do you bring it to life and transform these words and intentions into outcomes? This transformation process – the operationalisation of the mission – begins with the next decision area: determining what is in scope and what is out of scope. The mission statement will have defined or at least implied the learning function's field of responsibility, but the next task is to explicitly agree some specific boundaries. If your mission is a compass bearing telling you which way to go, your statement of scope is an instrument of clarity, a sextant with which you can check if you really are on course.

To facilitate boundary creation, the learning function must take three key decisions. It must identify the target populations within the business for whom it will provide services (its customers). It must decide for each group what the strategically relevant learning objectives will be (its deliverables). And it must determine what its relationship will be with any other learning systems, structures or personnel in place in the business (its interfaces). Without these decisions, it can be almost impossible to ensure strong alignment between the learning function's mandate (what it is supposed to be doing) and its learning scope (what it ends up doing).

Defining who: the target populations

The first decision deals with the *who* question: who in the company will the learning function provide services to? Defining your target groups involves dividing the whole population into subgroups and then deciding which you want to target. This may sound simple and obvious, but there are a number of different ways to approach the task. It can be likened to cutting a cake: the shape, size and types of pieces you end up with depend on how you approach slicing it up. The risk here for learning functions is that because both individuals and the business at large tend to have a traditional or favoured way of identifying the subgroups in the overall population, learning leaders and functions may take this as a given and not question or explore the value of doing it in a different way.

One possible division is simply distinguishing between internal employees and external customers and suppliers. IBM, for example, markets and sells a version of some of its internal technical training to external customers. Another way of cutting the cake is by job family or specialism. VW Coaching, for instance, which is deeply rooted in the German *Fachkompetenz* (professional competence) tradition, has structured part of its learning offer along the lines of what it calls 'professional families'. Learning is available for people in these groups from the lowest to the highest level and the offer includes both technical and non-technical professional skills. Similarly, Banco Santander has highly structured learning pathways leading to internal certification for people in certain specialisms and functions. Indeed, in some companies the prominence of technical and functional groups as target populations has led to the appearance of formal functional academies or schools that draw in leading specialists and enable the accumulation and sharing of knowledge and expertise. As we will see in Chapter 4, new learning technologies are today enabling more informal knowledge-sharing academies, too, in the shape of online 'communities of practice'.

Whatever form it takes, the advantage of a job family approach is that the target populations are defined on the basis of distinctive competencies that are seen as crucial to the organisation's success, creating strong alignment between the learning offer and organisational needs. The challenge with this approach, however, is that as the functional learning offers grow to encompass not only job-specific technical skills but also general professional skills, overlap and duplication can creep in between the job families.

Probably the most common way of cutting the cake, though, is by level. It tends to be the default approach either because different levels are viewed as having different development needs or because limited resources require some strategic decisions to be made about which group receives the most input. Whatever the driver is, the first group to stand out and be recognised as separate is almost always the executive population. With few exceptions, senior executives are seen as the most important target audience, and in fact some learning functions begin life purely focused on this group.

Another driver of the level approach is the need for talent management and nurturing a cadre of future leaders who 'belong' to the corporate centre. The main challenge here is that the lines dividing the remits of the talent management and corporate learning functions are often not clear, with the result being considerable potential for overlap. In our experience, where exactly the dividing line between the two functions is drawn is less significant than how it is subsequently lived. Tensions will inevitably arise and it is important that they are resolved not through political turf war, but with an eye to the overall strategic picture and longer-term consequences.

Finally, almost all corporate learning functions sooner or later face pressure or the opportunity to expand their coverage. Often this happens in response to the simple question of what should be done for those frontline or first-level managers who are not included in the leadership and talent groups. Although such expansion may be inevitable, it is often not easy, with the large middle and junior management populations usually being most difficult to integrate. The challenge here is both logistical and political. On the logistical side, the field of stakeholders that must be managed is exponentially bigger than with the smaller executive and talent groups, and the sheer size of the interface with the general management population usually demands a structure and processes for managing this relationship through a system of local learning managers, or through local HR or line managers. So purely logistically, taking this population on is not easy. But there is a political dimension too: often emotive and entrenched territorial reactions come to bear, driven by fear of losing control and budgetary battles. We shall come back to this issue later, but suffice to say for the moment that these reactions often exist and can be tricky.

Of course, in many businesses, target populations are defined by both job family and level, creating a rather complex cake. However you distinguish your customers, though, the important thing is to be aware of how you are doing it, and how you are not doing it. There is no one 'correct' way, but in order to make a deliberate choice, you should be aware of your options.

Defining what: the learning outcomes
The question that inevitably accompanies the *who* is the *what*: the objectives of learning. This will sometimes correspond directly to the target populations, for instance one set of programmes for executives and another for middle managers. But this does not always happen, and if it doesn't, the risk of misalignment can be significant. The point here is that you need to be clear about how the two sets of priorities – target populations and learning outcomes – align both with each other and with the mandated learning mission.

To help visualise your scope, it can be useful to draw a simple graph, with on one axis the *who*, the target population, and on the other axis the *what*, the intended learning objectives. This simple representation provides a strategic learning matrix that graphically shows your stakeholders exactly what is and is not in scope.

A possible complication is that the body identifying learning priorities is often not the same for all target groups. It may be the corporate centre when it comes to executive development, but when it comes to basic managerial or technical competencies, individual business units tend to make the decisions about what should be learned. In this case – and in fact in all cases – the learning function's task is to ensure that it does not get pulled into delivering something that, however good and valuable it may be, strays from the intent of its mandated mission. Because the weaker the alignment between mission and scope, the greater the risk that the function will struggle to add value to the organisation.

One further point here is to keep it simple and try to minimise the number of distinct learning objectives as far as possible. Changing behaviour is tough enough in the best of circumstances. To maximise your chances of success, you must be able to send an unambiguous message to people about what you want them to do, and one of the best ways to ensure this is not to send them lots of different messages. In fact, if you can encourage people to do just one thing differently each year, and that one thing impacts performance positively, you can consider it a success. It is far better to have one main annual learning objective, and to absolutely achieve it and drive it home, than to have five or six and achieve mediocre success with all.

Defining how: the learning function's role in the global learning landscape

One of the most difficult challenges in determining the scope of the central learning function's remit is its relationship to other learning structures, processes and personnel that may be in place across the business. Obviously, the bigger the business, the bigger this challenge is liable to be. In some smaller businesses, it may not be an issue at all. But for most learning functions it can present some tricky choices and negotiations, and it is liable to recur whenever the function's activity expands or changes.

Often a drive for centralisation, a desire to coordinate, standardise or rationalise, can come to bear in the relationship. The point of tension is that divisions and business units, which may be fiefdom-like geographical entities or may even once have been separate companies, tend to be reluctant to relinquish control over learning activity. In their efforts to construct a globally integrated learning offering, learning functions can thus find themselves on the ragged edge of a far bigger centralisation–decentralisation debate. And here I offer a word of caution for CLOs having to decide whether or not to go down this route. They need to be certain that they have the mandate to do so, the resources to do so effectively, and the influence required to manage the inevitable political tensions that will arise.

Moreover, it is not unusual for the move towards learning centralisation to happen in an uncoordinated or informal manner, without formal commitment from senior executives. When this happens there is a real risk of the learning function being drawn outside its mission or beyond the authority of its mandate and, more often than not, thence into difficulty. So it is critical that any steps towards centralisation are deliberate, overt and supported at an executive level.

It is important to remember, too, that the decision facing most learning functions is not usually an all-or-nothing, centralise or decentralise, choice; more often it is a question of degree and which bits to centralise and which bits to leave decentralised. Across the spectrum from full centralisation (which is rare) to a loose coordinating structure, there are many positions a company can choose. As an example, consider Figure 2.2, which describes four different levels of centralisation that can be achieved.

In this vein, one of the first and critical steps many learning functions take in defining this aspect of scope is to create a guiding coalition: a federating body (often called the Learning Board or Learning Council) made up of learning representatives from across the organisation. The purpose of this body is to discuss and agree to what extent and how centralisation, standardisation or coordination might happen, thus defining the nature of the central learning function's relationship to the broader business.

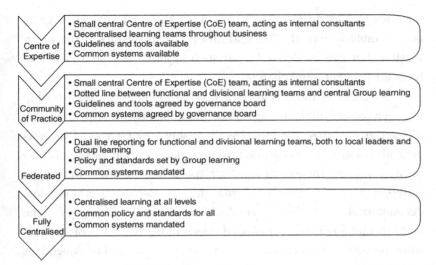

Centre of Expertise
- Small central Centre of Expertise (CoE) team, acting as internal consultants
- Decentralised learning teams throughout business
- Guidelines and tools available
- Common systems available

Community of Practice
- Small central Centre of Expertise (CoE) team, acting as internal consultants
- Dotted line between functional and divisional learning teams and central Group learning
- Guidelines and tools agreed by governance board
- Common systems agreed by governance board

Federated
- Dual line reporting for functional and divisional learning teams, both to local leaders and Group learning
- Policy and standards set by Group learning
- Common systems mandated

Fully Centralised
- Centralised learning at all levels
- Common policy and standards for all
- Common systems mandated

FIGURE 2.2 Four levels of centralisation

For example, one of the most common integration activities is to create a core curriculum shared across all areas of the business, in order to ensure shared learning experiences, create economies of scale and set minimum standards. A related choice is to what degree the organisation's overall catalogue of learning offerings should be rationalised. This can be particularly beneficial in larger organisations with a history of decentralised activity. To cite one striking example, Siemens has managed to reduce its overall portfolio from around 3,000 programmes to 200. Another consideration is whether and how to set up preferred external supplier lists and standardise processes for evaluating bids and contracting out. I shall return to this issue in Chapter 5 when we look at the resourcing of corporate learning.

Other potential decision points can revolve around systems. For example, many organisations choose to create a global reporting system. Without such a system, in some organisations it can be almost impossible to arrive at any accurate figures for the number of programmes delivered or the total amount spent on learning. A related option is the centralisation of learning technology systems into a common system that can manage online content, course logistics and learning records. Although both options can involve considerable logistical, financial and political obstacles, the information that can be derived from such systems can be a powerful lever for influence and change.

So there is more than one way to manage the relationship between the central learning function and the other learning entities and activities across the business. Precisely how far you go towards centralisation will depend upon many factors, such as the culture of the company, the extent to which its various business lines have different learning traditions, and the micro-politics among key decision-makers. And whatever decisions are made, the ability of the CLO to make things happen will depend largely on his or her personal powers of persuasion, since implementation will be dependent upon buy-in.

Like defining your mission and mandate, determining your scope is a multi-layered and complex issue, which entails a series of choices that may not at first be obvious. They are, nonetheless, significant. In fact, all the signs are that they are set to become even more complex and important, too, as an increasing number of learning functions report budgetary pressures and being asked to do more with less, and as around half of all organisations report increasing integration between learning and other people-related activities such as talent management, organisational development and performance management.[7] As the traditional boundaries of scope become stretched and blurred, being clear about the choices you are and are not making is going to become increasingly critical and challenging.

Assessing your scope

Questions to ask yourself when identifying your scope

1. Have both the types of intervention and the target groups been clearly defined?
2. Are you clear how the target populations have been identified?

3. Are the defined target populations and activities firmly aligned with the learning function's mission and mandate?
4. Are priorities identified?
5. Are the target populations and activities defined firmly aligned with the business's strategic objectives?
6. Is the corporate learning function clear about what it will *not* do?
7. Does the defined scope allow the learning function to construct its portfolio of programmes and services effectively?
8. What degree of centralisation is required to deliver your learning mission?
9. Is there agreement among top executives as to the degree of centralisation required by your learning strategy?
10. What does not need to be centralised?
11. Have you identified potential members from each business unit for a guiding coalition?

Positioning the function

The third key decision area is the positioning of the corporate learning function in the organisational structure and thus the web of reporting lines and interfaces that tie it into the company's decision-making processes and operational systems. Admittedly, this is usually a given, something you inherit, rather than a choice. But it is included in the list of key decision areas because where the learning function sits will significantly impact its ability to fulfil its mandated mission and reach its scope. Yet because it is an inherited condition, it is often overlooked and therefore not actively managed as a core part of the learning strategy. The message here is that you need to be acutely aware of such inherited conditions and consciously and proactively manage and mitigate their impact as far as possible. In this regard, four key things stand out:

1. The learning function's position will affect its access to both executive level decision-makers and its principal target audiences within the company. In particular, the learning function is dependent on the influencing skills of the CLO and his or her personal access to the main spheres of influence in the company.

2. The learning function's ability to deliver depends to some extent on its perceived standing in the business, and its position will impact this insofar as it sends a strong message to the business about senior executives' commitment to learning and their expectations of it.

3. How the learning function is positioned and how its reporting lines are defined will impact the autonomy that it has to act.

4. No matter how clear and well-mandated its mission, the learning function is likely to encounter implementation problems if its positioning does not provide it with sufficient authority to act. Unclear positioning and fuzzy interfaces with other functions can, for example, severely handicap the learning function in pursuing all or part of its mission.

Although the position of the learning function in the organisational structure is often beyond your control, it is useful to be aware of the most typical positions.

Reporting directly to the board

This solution sometimes occurs when a new learning function is created, particularly when the CEO is the driving force behind the project, and involves the learning function reporting directly to the CEO. It has the advantage of giving the CEO, and in a broader sense the executive board, direct control over the strategic deployment of the learning function; it comes into its own when there is a transformational agenda.

One example of this model is Allianz Management Institute, whose focus in the beginning was on the top 900 leaders in the company. Initially positioned outside of HR, it had a direct reporting line to the CEO and the executive committee. This was intended to facilitate full strategic control by the top executive, with an executive committee member 'sponsoring' each programme and participating personally in its design and delivery. This tight organisation allowed the CEO a strong platform for communication with his most senior leaders and fostered loyalty and a sense of belonging to the company as a whole rather than to one of its component parts.

An argument that is sometimes put forward in favour of direct reporting to the board is that placing learning outside the HR structure raises its profile and prestige within the business. This positioning has its limitations, however. The learning function may be less able to interface effectively with other key functions, in particular HR. As a result, links with HR people management processes such as talent development, recruitment and succession planning may be more difficult to manage, risking a disconnect between these core processes and the learning offer. In addition, a direct-to-board reporting line can also make it more difficult to integrate learning provision across the business. There is also the risk that, as time goes by, the board's attention may not remain as close as in the early days. And, of course, the senior executive team may change, bringing risks for the previous CEO's creation. For all of these reasons, there is a tendency to reposition a direct-to-board learning organisation closer to HR after a few years of operation.

Reporting within the HR function

By far the most common positioning is for the learning function to report directly to HR. This has numerous advantages, most notably that sitting within HR, it is easier to link learning to other people processes. The reporting line through the head of HR can be an effective route to board level decision-making, although things are not always simple. There may, for instance, be problems if the CLO does not report directly to the head of HR. Indeed, it is critical that the learning function is not too far down the hierarchical ladder to be able to receive a clear strategic mandate from the top. In addition, by being positioned within HR, learning will inevitably inherit some of HR's reputation in the business, for better or for worse. Difficulties may surface, for example, when the HR function has not yet taken on a strategic business partner role in people development and remains heavily focused on traditional administrative and personnel management roles. In these cases it can be difficult for learning to be perceived as anything other than a reactive service function.

Reporting within another central function

This is the rarest of the three main positions and, in my experience, potentially the most problematic. For example, in a multinational insurance business I worked with, the learning function was placed within the Strategy and Innovation unit, whose head was one of the most influential senior managers in the company and, in the early days, a champion of the new learning initiative. However, as new priorities began to emerge and attention shifted to other projects, the learning function was left adrift without adequate support. It also had the impossible mission of trying to sell the idea of a new position for itself in another part of the organisation. In such a situation the function's autonomy, authority and access to executive decision-makers are at risk.

So there is no perfect place to be, but it is important to be clear about where you are and what the impact of this will be.

Assessing your positioning

Questions to ask yourself when considering the impact of your positioning

1. Does the positioning of the corporate learning function optimise its ability to fulfil its mission?
2. Does the learning function have adequate access to senior executives?
3. Does the learning function have adequate access to the key target populations within its scope?
4. Does the CLO's reporting line facilitate effective decision-making?
5. How does the learning function's positioning impact its visibility and perceived legitimacy within the company?
6. How does the learning function's positioning impact its autonomy and authority to operate?
7. Does the learning function have an effective interface with HR processes, both at corporate level and in the business units?
8. Is the learning function's interface with talent management well defined?

Choosing an operating model

The fourth decision area is a big one: namely, the operating model that the learning function chooses. 'Operating model' here refers to the internal design, processes and systems that it adopts – the foundations of its operations. The key question for the learning function, the critical decision it must make, is 'What business are we in?' Simply put, in order to excel at what you do, you need to be clear about what it is that you are doing. And we are not talking about specific objectives, programmes or processes. We are talking about how you create value for the organisation.

Of course, ultimately, all learning functions are in the same business, that of helping organisations to make money through performance support and improvement. Sooner or later, all that you do should result in the improved performance of individuals and the business. But there is, as the old adage goes, more than one way to skin a cat. And how you envisage the learning function's value creation role in the organisation will have significant implications for how it should be structured and organised.

For example, if you are responsible for the delivery of hundreds of technical training programmes, your operational model will need to be like that of a manufacturing or retail business. Your function is likely to resemble a training factory that will focus on ensuring quality at volume, making efficiencies and delivering economies of scale. Conversely, if you are mainly focused on organisational development and the facilitation of change, you will be operating more like an internal consulting unit. And if neither is the case and your focus is on the delivery of executive development, then your operating model will probably have a lot of similarities with that of a business school.

A clear value proposition is thus the foundation upon which any successful operating model is built. Unfortunately, this kind of basic clarity is missing in all too many organisations.

Identifying your value proposition

So what is the business that you are in, as a learning function? What is your value proposition? There are many frameworks to help identify optimal operating models, but we suggest thinking about it in terms of four simple and basic roles that learning functions can play (see Figure 2.3). All functions are likely to fulfil at least one of these roles and some may undertake them all. The critical challenge for learning leaders is to decide which of these roles their function will play; to recognise that they require different structures, cultures and skills to be successful; and to organise and resource their function accordingly.

Producer (selling the development of learning products) Probably the most common way for learning functions to create value is by developing learning products that can be provided or sold to customers across the business (e.g. like a car manufacturer). Typically, this involves the learning function creating a piece of training, which an external supplier or a local internal team then delivers.

Distributor (selling the delivery of learning products) Another common role is to take existing learning products, sometimes created by external suppliers, and organise the distribution and delivery of these products to customers (e.g. like a supermarket). It is common for this role to be combined with that of a Producer, but some learning functions play only the role of Distributor. The role is experiencing considerable change at the moment, as businesses continue to look for more cost-effective ways to deliver learning content[8] and, as an increasing number of them are doing, expand learning delivery to include customers and partners.[9]

Provider (selling support services) The third role is a bit different. The previous two involved selling some form of product to customers (the design of learning products or their delivery). Infrastructure providers, by contrast, create value by developing and lending out the right to use infrastructure or support processes (e.g. like a rail network). Some learning functions provide the infrastructure for learning to take place across the organisation, for instance by operating bricks-and-mortar learning centres or providing IT systems. In these scenarios, the learning function usually retains ownership of the infrastructure and can regulate its use. So when, as often happens, learning functions provide administrative and project management support, they tend to retain the headcount while lending out the resource. Few learning functions operate in the Provider role alone, but an increasing number of them are taking it on as an additional service.

Broker (selling consulting services, knowledge and advice) The final role is brokerage, in which the value created comes from matching service providers with customers (e.g. like a real estate agency). This role typically involves learning managers acting as internal consultants, partnering with business units, leaders and teams to help diagnose their learning need and then providing internally or externally developed learning solutions to meet it.

The biggest challenges in identifying the role you play tend to be a lack of clear scope and, less obviously, personal bias in the form of the CLO's preferences. It is important to explicitly and as objectively as possible think through how your learning function will go about fulfilling its mission and add value to the organisation. Moreover, once you are clear, you need to employ a healthy dose of what we like to call *functionalism*.

The glory of functionalism
As words go, 'functionalism' does not sound the most exciting, and certainly not the type to be found alongside 'glory'. This is a shame, because from my work with businesses, I am convinced that a *functionalist* approach to corporate learning is critical to success. As dry as the word may sound, it has an immensely practical focus: it simply refers to the idea that the design of something should match its required function – what it is intended to do. This is important because no matter how good the quality of a learning function's programmes and how competent its staff, it will not and cannot achieve its mandated mission unless its structure, processes and systems are all effectively

Producer	Distributor
Selling the development of learning products	Selling the delivery of learning products

Provider	Broker
Selling support services	Selling consulting services, knowledge and advice

FIGURE 2.3 What business are you in?

aligned both with one another and with the core purpose of the function. This may sound blatantly obvious, but in my experience it is too
often assumed or overlooked and not explicitly considered.

Three of the main considerations here are the learning function's people, structure and business model. I'll go on to explore the
resourcing of the learning function in Chapter 5, but for the moment I
will focus on aligning the function's structure and business model.

Choosing a structure What are the basic, common structural configurations for learning functions? Intuitively, one might think
there would be some, or at least one, semi-standard model that many
functions adopt. Yet strikingly, amazingly, there aren't. Indeed, the
functions I have observed have a bewildering variety of internal
structures, with each business inventing its own solution. So there
are no basic, common structural configurations. The upside of this is
that there is complete latitude for creativity in adapting your structure to operational requirements. The downside, though, is that
in the absence of standard configurations, when leaders inevitably
change or functions are restructured, the pieces continually seem to
fall in different ways, leading to a lack of continuity.

As a basic guide, although there are no 'standard' structures,
there do seem to be standard components. For example, many structures I have seen have a team responsible for programme design and
delivery, generally supported by a separate team responsible for the
Learning Management System (LMS) or other IT applications. There

is also often a team responsible for logistics and event management, and some learning functions have people in business partner-like roles as well, to interface with key internal customer groups.

One common structure created from these components is to have a central 'centre of expertise' group, comprising design, IT and administrative teams, with geographically based teams playing delivery and business partner roles. An alternative structure involves the learning function organising its services according to major internal clients in the business, each with its own 'centre of expertise'. The Capgemini University is a good example of this, with seven specialised schools, four of which correspond to the company's main business lines: the Consulting School, the Technology School, the Business Development School and the Outsourcing School. The Leadership Development School is responsible for cross-divisional, corporate level programmes aimed at Capgemini's executive population, while the remaining two schools cover the finance sector and the learning needs of a subsidiary business.

The key message here is not to be led by personal bias or the pressure of what already exists or what exists elsewhere, to take nothing as a given, and to take the time to step back and start the design process objectively. This may sound a tad unhelpful to some, but the point is that although there is no 'right' way to guide you, there is also no 'right' way to constrain you, and you should be led by the needs of the situation you face rather than by any model.

Choosing a business model A further potentially difficult decision, with significant political and practical consequences, is choosing your business model. This is sometimes oversimplified as a choice between a profit/breakeven model, in which programme costs are charged as fees to the participants' business units, and a cost centre model in which learning costs are part of a central corporate budget. Yet the situation is rarely this simple, and many learning functions use a hybrid system, with some learning initiatives funded centrally and others charged back to the business units.

GDF Suez University, for example, which is formally listed as a limited company, operates a hybrid model in which corporate programmes for senior executives and the talent pipeline are charged to a central corporate cost centre, while the broader portfolio of programmes are charged back to participants' business units. Capgemini, by contrast, operates a straight not-for-profit charge-back model, with course fees being billed to participants' business units. Novartis, meanwhile, does pretty much the opposite, with programmes and services in large part funded centrally. And, as a final example, Siemens defines its learning unit as a profit centre and charges back to the business units not only participants' fees but also consulting and project fees.

In my experience, which model businesses choose tends to be driven by immediate logistics and what seems easiest at the time. But I would urge you to look further, because although the longer-term practical implications of which model you choose are often not recognised, they can nonetheless be significant. For example, with a centrally funded programme, the learning function tends to be primarily concerned with delivering a high-quality product that satisfies participants and convinces executives of its value. When costs are charged back to the business units, however, the situation is very different. Satisfaction and value are still essential, but filling programmes can become key (in order to cover costs) and, by extension, issues such as pricing, marketing and ability to respond to participants' needs will also become more relevant. Opening the learning function to some market pressures has the advantage of making its staff more alert to such customer-related issues, but it also makes the function more vulnerable to factors beyond its control.

So the choice of business model is about more than just how programmes are funded. Indeed, whether you are selecting staff, choosing a structure or deciding on a funding model, it is important to be aware of the broader implications and strive to ensure functionalism between these elements of your operating model and your value proposition. Ultimately, ensuring functionalism can be tricky and something that requires careful forethought. It also requires even more careful rethinking, as one of the most difficult challenges that learning functions face as they expand their scope is first to recognise and then to deal with the fact that their operating model may not be optimal for their new scope. One issue that I see an increasing number of functions face, for example, is the roles of staff expanding as the function grows, to the point at which they might incorporate everything from acting as consultants and looking at the strategic big picture to the micro-level of closing individual skill gaps. As most people are not able to operate on so many different levels, they can end up overstretched, and as a result their clients' perceptions of their competence and contribution can be tainted.

Since there are few if any guiding rules, the main point is for learning leaders to constantly question themselves about how the learning structure aligns with the role it plays and to be aware of the advantages and disadvantages associated with the solutions they choose. Yet again, the key is to be conscious of your choices and pro-active and purposeful in making them.

Assessing your operating model

Questions to ask yourself when considering your learning operating model

1. Are you clear what business you are in? What is your value proposition? Is this aligned to your mandated mission?
2. In what ways does the internal organisation of the learning function help and hinder the achievement of its main objectives?
3. Is this internal structure aligned with the learning function's scope?
4. Is this structure consistent with the structure of the overall programme portfolio?
5. Is the business model aligned with the learning function's purpose and mission?
6. Does the learning function's business model facilitate effective operations with regard to planning, budgeting and client interface?
7. Does the operating model allow for innovation and experimentation?

Building a portfolio

The final decision area in the map for building an aligned learning strategy revolves around constructing a portfolio of programmes and services. In the next chapter I explore the development of individual learning initiatives; here the focus is on the overall logic of the portfolio, on the quality of the portfolio as a whole rather than of individual programmes. The question here is not so much 'Are we doing things right?' as 'Are we doing the right things?'

I am aware that many learning functions' portfolios are at least partly emergent: they develop over the course of the business year as new learning needs arise. But most learning functions formulate an annual learning plan – usually in conjunction with annual budgets – and this is my focus here. It is a critical process because, like your operational model, it links together the strategic objectives of your mandated mission with the operational processes that your function delivers: it links what you are supposed to be doing with what you end up doing.

In developing or reviewing a portfolio plan, there are three key decisions that have to be considered: what to prioritise in the portfolio, how to structure it and how to present it.

What to prioritise in the portfolio

This is at once both simple and complex. It is simple because decisions relating to what to prioritise should be driven by your mandated mission and defined scope, as well as the broader objectives of the business. It can get complex, though, because life is rarely that simple, and budgeting and political considerations are almost bound to come into play – rarely to positive effect. Another consideration is alignment of the central learning function's activity with that of any other learning teams across the company. Half the challenge here is to be accurately informed about what is happening and planned elsewhere; the other half is to avoid turf wars. Suffice to say, the key objective of the learning function is not to be pulled off course: to retain a consistent focus on the mandated mission. If there is significant demand for objectives that lie outside the mission, they can be discussed, but they should not be pursued without a mandated change to the mission. I return to this issue in Chapter 3 and look at how learning functions can retain the coherence and consistency of their learning portfolio in the face of ad hoc requests for learning from the business. For the moment, however, what is important is that when the learning plan goes before senior executives and the broader business, all who see it will recognise it as a coherent offering that reflects the agreed strategic remit of the learning function.

How to structure the portfolio

In my experience, this second question of how to structure the portfolio tends to be less explicitly considered. The key issue here is how to create a coherent framework for grouping programmes and services. The most common solution is to use the target groups identified in the defining scope process as the basis for the portfolio's structure. For each customer group (e.g. executive management, talent pipeline high potentials, and middle management), the programmes and services to be provided are shown, typically in the form of a matrix that puts the target groups on one axis and the learning initiatives on the other. So far, so easy.

As when defining your scope, though, the lines you draw can have some unexpected consequences. Take, for example, one of the most common distinctions made, between leadership development and management development. Although this sounds innocuous enough, what usually happens when grouping the portfolio around such target groups is that there is an underlying and often unconscious tendency to accentuate the differences between the groups – to show that you have a unique offering for each. For example, leadership development is typically focused more on 'softer' and high-level skills, such as self-awareness and strategic thinking, while middle management development emphasises operational skills, such as managing people. Yet although it is true that business leaders manage businesses whereas managers manage people, the distinctions between the two types of role are often more blurred than this simple stereotype and the learning portfolios of many businesses would suggest: leaders also have to manage, and managers with responsibility for other people's work must lead to some extent. Yet by constructing the portfolio around the target groups identified in the scoping process, learning functions may inadvertently create distinctions between these groups that are more artificial than real.

I strongly recommend that you do *not* automatically construct your portfolio around the same target groups you identified when defining the learning function's scope. Rather, instead of using the *who* of your scope as the basis for your portfolio, I suggest you use the *what* – the key learning objectives you have identified. For example, if your key strategic objectives are to improve the quality of performance management conversations and improve the degree of intellectual challenge in the organisation, then I suggest you structure the portfolio around these objectives and list for each one the groups you will target and the programmes you will offer. The advantage of this approach is that it makes it easier to ensure that the portfolio addresses your mandated mission. I would still suggest producing a traditional matrix of target groups and offerings as this can be useful to assess the level of balance in the portfolio and because it is probable that business leaders will want to know what offerings will be available for each of these groups. It is important not to think merely in terms of coverage; you should also consider impact and what you are trying to achieve.

How to present the portfolio

To be honest, there is not much to say here beyond the fact that the learning function needs to be able to provide the organisation with a readable overview of the portfolio. I am saying it, nonetheless, because all too often I have observed serious shortcomings in the communication of portfolios. This may be partly due to poor marketing or to constantly changing visualisations of the offer, but in my experience, a basic lack of clarity on how best to structure the portfolio more often than not lies at the heart of the matter. The articulation and visualisation of the portfolio is a fundamental communication tool that, as much as any logo (see Chapter 7), says something about the learning function and its role in the business, both internally within the learning function and externally to the function's customers and stakeholders across the wider organisation.

So building a portfolio can be both simple and complex. And of course once it is built, the story is not over, as it will need evaluating, reviewing and rebuilding on a regular basis. The essential is that it provides a clear and direct answer to the basic question 'Are we doing the right things?'

Assessing your portfolio

Questions to ask yourself when considering your learning portfolio

1. Is the portfolio optimally aligned with both the mandated mission of the learning function and its defined scope?
2. Does the portfolio fully reflect the current learning priorities of the organisation?
3. Are there gaps in the portfolio in terms of types of learning provision (e.g. are there groups for whom there is little or no available learning)?
4. How coherent is the overall portfolio?
5. How well is the portfolio of programmes aligned with the offering of other providers within the company?
6. Have you avoided duplications in the programme portfolio?
7. Is the programme portfolio presented in a readable fashion and easily understood by people across the company?

CONCLUDING THOUGHTS

As we have seen, the map of how to build a learning strategy and align the learning function behind it includes five decision areas that must be thought through. For when crafted well, strategy becomes a tool that can slice through complexity. This brings us to the nub of the issue: crafting it well is far from easy and, sometimes, as the spaghetti-facing CLO found out, it is just not possible. Indeed, the reality for many learning functions is that imperfections will remain: places where clarity or a unified mandate is not achievable given the logistical and political landscapes. Yet an effort must be made.

My aim in providing this map has not been to offer a detailed description and debate of the many intricacies of strategy formation, but to highlight the major decision points that can impact the coherence and alignment of a learning strategy. And my message is the need to seize this task wholeheartedly – purposefully and pro-actively – with a functionalist mindset and an eye to both the past and the future.

I say the past because, in my experience, the key challenge that learning leaders face in developing an aligned learning strategy is the weight of history: the traditions and assumptions that guide how we see and understand the tasks before us, and thus the decisions we make. Not only are these ties to the past difficult to recognise, but they can make it challenging to see where key decision points lie and what our options are. The well-trodden path may well be the best for a business, but it must never be assumed to be such.

And I say the future because without a successfully aligned strategy, it is hard to see what future a learning function can have beyond that of a reactive service provider. If corporate learning functions are to add value, and to be seen to be doing so, they need to have a mandated plan for doing so. Of course, aligning the various elements of a learning strategy is only the beginning because it then has to be delivered. And it is to this operationalisation of strategy that I now turn, beginning with the development of learning initiatives.

3 Developing learning solutions: linking learning objectives with the methods used to achieve them

So you have a strategy, and an aligned one at that. So far, so good. Now you have to do something about it. If you aren't worried, you should be. Because, as I have noted, there is something about what we are doing that is not producing the results that businesses want. The lack of clear, mandated strategies is likely to be part of the reason, but it is not the whole story. Indeed, in the search for what is at fault, any line-up of usual suspects is likely to contain the elements of development and design – how learning solutions are developed and put together. This seems reasonable, for as with any product you buy, if it does not do the job it is supposed to, then faulty design is a judicious assumption.

In this chapter we look at whether concerns about the development of learning solutions are justified and, if so, what is going wrong and what can be done about it. A framework is provided for learning leaders to examine the effectiveness of how learning solutions are developed in their own business and in doing so examine the process through which learning needs are identified. I also show that there is some confusion between methods/tools (delivery) and desired outcomes of learning solutions. I deal with the former in more depth in Chapter 4. In this chapter, as with the previous chapter, my intention is not to provide a detailed how-to guidebook filled with directions about which turns to take where, but to provide a framework within which the various challenges can be identified, options can be assessed and decisions made. And, as with the previous chapter, it is a story of the power of functionalism.

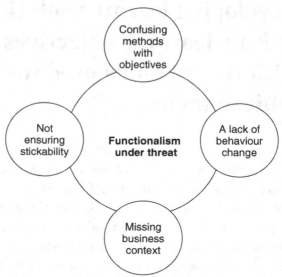

FIGURE 3.1 Functionalism under threat

FOUR HIDDEN THREATS

Functionalism, as I have already noted, refers to the idea that the design of a particular thing should match what it is intended to do. In the context of developing learning solutions, this simply means that the technologies, content and methods used in the learning solution should enable the learning objectives to be achieved. I would be pretty surprised if anyone reading this disagreed with it. Yet a lack of functional alignment can be difficult to spot; it is far from obvious. Indeed, I believe that there are four ways in which functional alignment in the development of corporate learning solutions has been, and remains, subtly but fundamentally undermined (see Figure 3.1).

Confusing methods and tools with objectives

In thinking about learning, about what it is and how it works, it is hard not to think of and be informed by personal experiences of school and academic-based learning. Yet learning in the corporate environment is a rather different beast. One of the main differences is that in academic learning, the very process of learning is often viewed as a valuable objective. In corporate learning, however, learning is not generally an end product in itself, but is merely a means to an end – a process through which an outcome that is of value to individuals and organisations can be produced. At least, that's the theory.

The history of corporate learning, however, is littered with examples of where greater focus has been placed on the learning processes and methods used than on learning objectives and outcomes, to the extent that these processes have been seen as end products in themselves.[10] Many readers will be able to think of at least one or two examples of where such an emphasis on programmes as end products has occurred. Indeed, a common caricature of corporate learning delivery is that it is more interested in delivering programmes than delivering value to the business.

The first response of some people on reading this may be that it is a thing of the past – a description of corporate learning as it was twenty or thirty years ago. Yet for a very modern example, look no further than blended learning, originally conceived as an approach to design.[11] Blended learning concerns the use of different pedagogies – teaching methods – and in particular the use of instructor-centred and learner-centred means. As an approach to design, it can improve the accessibility of learning, enrich the learning process by engaging a variety of learning styles, and afford cost savings through less time spent in the classroom.[12] Unsurprisingly, it has captured the attention of many organisations as a versatile, effective approach to learning delivery and is one of the key current trends in corporate learning.

Yet as a quick Google search reveals, blended learning is commonly not seen as a design method or approach but as a product or solution in itself. In fact, though it is not dependent on technology and even pre-dates much current technology as an approach, it has become seen as a technology-related product, synonymous with the use of e-learning.[13] As subtle and innocuous as this mislabelling may seem, it confuses the means with the end and so draws our eyes from our real objectives. Indeed, in this vein, as I will explore in more depth in Chapter 4, I believe that many of the wonderful new technologies becoming available to us represent not only exciting opportunities but also very real threats. This is partly because providers have understandably tried to productise their offerings in an effort to differentiate themselves and achieve competitive advantage. Whatever the cause, when such methods and tools are dangled before us like shiny, desirable products, they appear attractive and valuable in their own right, especially to some business leaders, and thus distract us and them from looking more closely at how these products align with the value that our learning needs to produce. Given the glittering array of technological wonders available, keeping focus and not confusing our means with our end has never been more difficult.

Failing to focus on behaviour change and the application of learning

A second influence of the traditional, academic view of learning is that it has led corporate learning professionals to talk and think about corporate learning as either the accumulation of knowledge or the acquisition of skills. But viewing learning this way misses the point that it is not the skills or knowledge per se but how they are applied that provides value to organisations. Sooner or later, one way or another, much of corporate learning boils down to changing people's behaviour in ways that produce value for the business.

We need to pause here because I want to be clear. I am aware that in some European countries companies have a legal obligation to provide training and continuing education for their employees and that this may sometimes resemble education in the traditional academic sense. I am also aware that much technical training resembles traditional academic learning. And I am convinced that there is undoubtedly a time and a place for traditional academic learning in organisations and that it can add value. But I also want to recognise the reality that in most organisations in most countries, most of the learning offered to employees is provided with a specific end in mind, which either directly involves or eventually leads to a change in behaviour and improvement in performance. My concern is that the lack of reference to behaviour change is starkly misaligned with this reality.

So absent is behaviour from the equation that if we ask the average designer of corporate learning solutions to outline his or her theory of behaviour change, we are likely to get a response that goes no further than mentioning differences in learning styles. And I continue to be surprised that fields that have a great deal to say about how to change people's behaviour, such as behaviour economics and even psychotherapy, are so little referred to and drawn upon for ideas and inspiration. Of course, the gap that behaviour change fills has not gone unnoticed, and in fact it is one of the most researched and discussed aspects of learning delivery. However, it is not referred to as behaviour change, but as the transfer of training. This may sound like semantics, a difference in name only. But words matter. The language of 'transfer of training' engenders a line of thinking and the consideration of issues that are quite different from the ones that would be raised if we talked of behaviour change.

One reason the concept of behaviour change is a rarity may be that it sounds unfashionable or distasteful, in that the phrase carries with it a political undercurrent, a suggestion of coercion or manipulation. I certainly wouldn't advise renaming your chief learning officer the 'director of behaviour change' or, even worse, the 'director of behaviour modification'. Yet I believe that the lack of discussion of behaviour change as an issue has had a significant and fundamentally negative impact on the field of corporate learning. The challenge of changing behaviour is not the same as the challenge of imparting information or teaching skills, and not talking about it prevents us from raising and recognising these different challenges. In joining the dots between learning objectives, methods and outcomes, behaviour change is a missing link – one without which we cannot create functional alignment.

Failing to promote stickability

If the lack of behavioural focus has limited the breadth of discussions about learning, another issue has limited their length – or, more specifically, the period of time considered worth discussing. A common way of conceptualising the various stages in learning delivery is the ADDE model: analysis, design, delivery and evaluation. It contains the implicit idea that once learning or training has been designed and then delivered, it is pretty much over, except for the evaluation. So it views learning as a one-off event and thus often assumes that it has a one-off impact and return on investment as well. We send person A on a sales training course, she finishes it, and we expect her sales figures to have improved at year-end as a result. Full stop.

A longitudinal perspective is absent here. So we have been missing the issue not only of how to change behaviour but also of how to keep that behaviour changed. One of the first case studies on why this is so important was published in the 1950s and examined the impact of training on manufacturing foremen at International Harvester Company.[14] Immediately after training, almost all the foremen demonstrated the required behaviour change, but after several months most had returned to their original behaviour. Further studies have replicated these findings and it is now pretty well established that skills learned during training will usually show some 'decay', as they fall into disuse over time.[15] If we take this into consideration and adopt a longitudinal perspective, person A goes on a sales training course and we then use a mixture of incentives and reinforcement techniques to help ensure that the skills learned are replicated not only this year but also next. And as a result, the return on investment is seen not as a one-off return but as a continuing one.

The issue is not totally ignored, however. Indeed, as a concept it is increasingly mentioned – as the 'stickability' of learning – but again it is talked of in terms of knowledge and how best to retain it, not in terms of behaviour. As a result, modern corporate learning lacks much discussion on how to ensure the reinforcement and replication of target behaviours. And when this piece of the puzzle is missing, it limits our ability to ensure functional alignment.

Missing business context

The fourth and final limiter of our ability to drive functional alignment is context or, more accurately, the lack of context. One of the most consistent findings arising from research into the transfer of training is the importance of contextual factors, commonly referred to as the 'learning climate', in enabling behaviour change and the application of learning.[16] Indeed, the research is clear that contextual factors, such as whether the workplace environment allows for learning to be applied and supports it, are actually *more* important in ensuring the application of learning than the quality of the training or learning event.[17]

The last sentence is worth rereading. It may surprise some readers, but in many learning programmes consideration of these issues appears little more than an afterthought. It is true that in recent years there has been a greater focus on these factors, in part because transferring 'home' practices to distant sites or foreign operations is a growing issue for many organisations. And Harvard Business School's Amy Edmondson has been highlighting the importance of contextual factors in how people learn and behave at work for the past twenty years, through her concept of *psychological safety*. Yet by and large, contextual factors are either ignored or boiled down and oversimplified into being only about the importance of the line manager in supporting learning. Given the historical focus on learning as imparting knowledge and skills to individuals, this lack of a systemic focus is perhaps not surprising. This failure to more fully consider systemic factors has significantly limited the ability of corporate learning functions to align these elements.

Moreover, the time-limited and relatively failure-intolerant nature of most workplace environments means that they are not naturally conducive to learning,[18] as evidenced by the enduring popularity of learning programmes that take employees out of the work setting. In fact, the criticality of this issue appears to be increasing as surveys suggest that corporate environments seem to be becoming even less learner-friendly. As organisations have de-layered, jobs have grown bigger and people have become busier. Recent findings suggest that around 40 per cent of people now say that they are 'excessively busy' at work, with half of middle managers reporting that their workloads have increased since the downturn began, and just over half of all employees reporting an increase in stress.[19] The modern business environment is certainly not at all suited to helping people to learn and then act upon this learning.

ENSURING ALIGNMENT

Together, these four historical issues have weighed heavily on the development of learning solutions, usually hidden and below the surface, but no less influential for that. Together, they continue to undermine and limit our ability to ensure that the design of learning solutions aligns with what the solutions are required to achieve. However obvious and simple this task sounds, for all the reasons mentioned above it often is not, and a dislocation of elements is common.

So let us now look at how we might avoid some of these issues, as well as at the process of developing learning solutions. This has traditionally been seen as involving two steps – needs analysis and design. Although this categorisation is logical, it reflects the traditional, academic approach more than the realities of value production in the corporate environment, because its structure and language lack a commercial approach. So I believe that the process of developing learning solutions needs to be reframed and rethought. Specifically, I suggest recasting it as a three-stage process (see Figure 3.2):

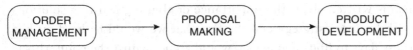

FIGURE 3.2 Three stages of producing corporate learning solutions

- Order management, which has not historically been seen as part of this process.
- Proposal making, which is partly what has more traditionally been called needs analysis, but also contains elements of design.
- Product development, which is similar in function to what has historically been called design.

Order management

Regardless of learning functions' chosen operational model – whether manufacturer, distributor or broker – a common challenge they all face is order management: how to handle requests for learning solutions. It is about deciding when they will say yes, and to what they will say no. Traditionally, this activity is viewed as part of the portfolio planning process covered in Chapter 2. Some organisations have strict annual portfolio planning processes, which do not allow for ad hoc requests for learning solutions through the year, and for these businesses, order management is indeed a once-per-year activity. In my experience, however, for the majority of businesses this is not the end of the matter. Yes there is a plan, but then additional requests occur, usually with the expectation that they will be serviced with solutions. As soon as this happens there is effectively a risk of being pulled off course and the portfolio may become inconsistent or misaligned. Indeed, I firmly believe that unless learning functions have a clear policy on the matter, it is inevitable that inconsistency and misalignment in the learning portfolio will sooner or later emerge.

Indications that order management is not a simple activity in many businesses can be found in the recent research showing that only 14 per cent of HR professionals believe that their current learning programmes are fully aligned with business needs.[20] Given the reams written about the importance of aligning learning solutions with business strategy and the fact that we would be hard pushed these days to find anyone who would argue against the point, this is quite a staggering finding. And it begs the question, 'What is going on?' From my experience, a lack of clear scope and a lack of an order management policy are the most common reasons for this misalignment. In fact I have seen too many learning functions without any such policy become overrun, bogged down by simply reacting to requests and never having the breathing space to think about them.

Yet for all its importance, order management is one of the most overlooked steps in corporate learning, one that is rarely mentioned. The reason for this is an historical hangover, an example of how corporate learning has been tied by traditions and is not as quick as it should be in adapting to changing times. Wind the clock back twenty years to when training functions were commonly viewed as responsive service functions, there to respond to the learning needs of the business. In these bygone days, the caricature of activity was that when a request came in, the learning function would leap into a needs analysis, to produce an objective study of the need and potential solutions, from which a decision about whether to proceed could be reached. To be honest, these days are not all bygone, but the world has turned and learning functions are trying to do more than merely provide a responsive service. To achieve this, though, they cannot respond to all requests willy-nilly; they need to have a policy or process that considers any request in the context of the overall mission, scope and portfolio.

So what should your order management policy look like? There is no single, best way of managing requests, but there are some key questions you need to answer:

1. *Will you have a formal process, or an informal one?* This is likely to be largely informed by your current business culture, but it is important because it sets the tone for the process. At one end of the spectrum, a formal process can involve the annual identification of key priorities, coordinated centrally, with business units providing requested

information in a structured and standardised way. At the other end of the spectrum, there is a completely informal, non-standardised and decentralised priority setting, with little or no data collection centrally. Each has its advantages and disadvantages. Too formal, and you can be seen as inflexible. Too informal, and it can be hard to monitor activity. Where you will sit in the spectrum requires careful thought.

2. *From where will you accept orders?* For example, will you accept orders at line manager level, or will you seek to funnel orders through learning representatives at business unit level? Obviously, your operational model and organisational and HR structures will be key issues in this decision.

3. *How will you decide which learning needs to prioritise?* For example, will it be a bottom-up process driven by the business, or a top-down process driven by the corporate agenda? This is the difference between order setting and order taking, and in practice it is likely that in most organisations a combination of the two will occur. Indeed, a careful balancing act is required, for without a degree of top-down perspective no alignment of learning investment is possible, yet without a degree of bottom-up influence, optimising these learning investments is equally challenging. Important influencers of this decision are likely to include organisational structure, the degree of centralisation and the way stakeholders are prioritised.

4. *Who will decide about what to prioritise and what not to?* Will decisions, for example, be made by the learning function or by an advisory group that represents the business? This issue is likely to be political as much as practical – and with good reason, for the decision-making process is an opportunity to obtain a mandate for action. As repeated studies have shown, when senior executives are involved in setting the learning agenda, these agendas are more likely to be viewed as being aligned with business needs and successful in delivering to them.[21]

5. *How often will decisions be taken?* If one end of the spectrum is simply to review learning needs and make decisions on an ad hoc basis, the other end of the spectrum is to review learning needs and requests at regular intervals, such as annually. The advantage of this approach is that it makes it easier to prioritise and to have a clear strategic direction. The disadvantage is that it will, by definition, make it more difficult to remain responsive to business needs. If you adopt this approach,

you need to consider the cycle times of your business. For example, one common approach is to align setting learning priorities with annual succession planning and/or the performance management cycle. However, some technology firms have product life cycles of just nine months, in which case an annual review makes little sense.

6. *What happens once a decision is made?* Should you prepare a needs analysis or proposal or, once the decision has been made, can you move straight to designing the learning offer? And if a needs analysis or proposal is necessary, who will it be presented to (for example, the CLO, the requesting client or an advisory group)? Likely influencers here are your current culture in terms of operating speed as well as the nature of the issue itself, since more careful thought may be required on how to proceed with some learning needs, whereas others are more straightforward.

So order management is a fundamental and too often overlooked issue in the operations of the corporate learning function. It is the key to maintaining your mission and staying in scope. It is the foundation upon which the development of learning solutions needs to be built, the basic decision about whether to develop something or not. And constructing anything without a firm foundation is rarely a wise move.

Assessing order management

Questions to ask yourself when developing an order management policy

1. To what extent will the process of order management be formal? If it is formal, what will mark it as such?
2. From where and whom will you accept orders? How does this align with the current HR and business structure? What, if any, exceptions could there be (e.g. particularly important stakeholders)?
3. To what extent will the setting of learning priorities be led by the centre? If it is set by the centre, to what extent will you allow or turn a blind eye to local learning activities?
4. Who will the decision-makers be? If you use an advisory group to set learning priorities, how do you ensure they approve ongoing requests?

5. How often will you set learning priorities?
6. How will the timing of decision-making align with the timing of other business and people processes? If you accept requests on an ad hoc basis, what will and will not qualify as a trigger for a decision?
7. Have you clearly articulated expectations of the next steps following decision-making and the conditions of any decisions made?

PROPOSAL MAKING

Once a potential learning issue has been identified, the next step traditionally taken in most organisations is some kind of needs analysis. This is a process through which the *what* and the *how* of a learning need or solution can be systematically identified. If an analysis occurs before a specific learning need has been identified then it is naturally more about what needs exist than about how to address them. If it happens in response to a specific request, then it is more about the how.

If we go back ten or twenty years, learning needs analysis was almost an industry in its own right. Book upon book has been written on the subject, many of which are not for the faint-hearted, or at least not for those of us who are not naturally inclined towards detail and process. These days, things are a bit different. Needs analysis is still seen as a critical cog, but it is not the industry it once was and the pressure is on learning functions to spend as little time as possible on it[22] and to 'bother' the business as little as possible with what can sometimes be seen as a purely technical activity. Hence the increasing use of the phrase 'rapid needs analysis',[23] an attempt to retain some of the rigour of old, but with an added sense of urgency.

Yet there has been a shift in how needs analysis is used. As business leaders have become more aware and knowledgeable about learning, and as learning functions have come closer to their businesses, needs analysis has been used less to identify learning needs and more to work out how to respond to already identified needs. Indeed, the function that it more frequently tends to perform these days is that of a project plan and proposal for how a learning need can be addressed.

If an organisation really is operating from a blank slate and requires someone to provide an objective view of learning needs, then a traditional needs analysis is still the way forward (which typically involves gathering as much data as possible on skills required and skill levels present and then analysing for gaps between the two). Otherwise, though, I would contend that the traditional concept of the needs analysis is outdated. To reflect its modern function, it needs to be recast as *proposal making*: the point at which a proposal for developing a solution to a learning need is generated. Recasting needs analysis as proposal generation repositions corporate learning activity as value creating and emphasises its commercial objectives. Again, I do not wish to stray into providing detailed guidance on how to write a learning proposal, but some broad guidelines do stand out:

1. *All good proposals should contain an element of archaeology*: an exploration of the identified learning need to see if learning *is* the required solution. In complex systems such as organisations, most performance problems have multiple causes and all too often corporate learning can find it is being asked to solve problems with root causes that have little to do with skill gaps. For example, in my experience it is not uncommon for a perceived skill gap to have less to do with individuals' ability levels and more to do with whether the business culture and/or reward structure enables, encourages and supports the expression of certain behaviours. It is imperative that if corporate learning functions are to establish and maintain their credibility they know their limitations, know what can and cannot be achieved, and are not tempted to take on something that cannot be delivered well, just to please a customer. Deciding what not to do is as important as deciding what to do.

2. *More haste, less speed*. The phrase, sometimes attributed to the Roman historian Suetonius, means that rushing into things without forethought can in fact slow them down. 'Rapid needs analysis' is all well and good, and in many businesses – especially those with a

strong operational focus – there are likely to be significant pressures to develop and implement the solution with great speed, but it is not worth skipping proposal making. Do it and do it right. If the proposal is not done right, the chances are that the subsequent product development will not be done right, and hence that objectives will not be achieved.

3. *How involved should the business be?* You have to walk a fine line between, on the one hand, involving the business in developing the proposal – for example, discussing feasibility issues – and, on the other hand, maintaining a position of objectivity and expertise. The challenge here is that proposal making is, like order management, more often than not a political task. The positive aspect is that it therefore also presents an opportunity to create political support and alignment for a particular solution. Indeed, a two-year-long study of the role of organisation politics in the proposal making process found that success at this stage largely depends on how corporate learning functions use data and technical expertise to educate and influence business leaders on the merits of particular approaches and solutions – a far cry from the traditional stereotype of the dry, intellectual and objective needs analysis. The political element of proposal making must not be forgotten and, indeed, should be central to it.

4. *How to change behaviour and keep it changed?* This is the biggest challenge that corporate learning faces, and the proposal should reflect this. It should, therefore, contain an element, or at least an understanding, of design, and a judgement on whether the behaviour change required is achievable, given any constraints that may be present. It should explicitly specify the intended behaviour change that will lead to performance improvements, as well as addressing both the contextual and longitudinal challenges of changing the behaviour and keeping it changed. This aspect of the proposal is critical because it makes clear what the learning function can do and emphasises what the business has to do to support and ensure that the learning has the intended impact. As a rule of thumb, if the proposal does not indicate responsibilities for both corporate learning and business leaders, it is likely that its analysis of the situation is incomplete. And simply stating the importance of business support for learning outcomes is not sufficient: the actual support required needs to be discussed, specified and agreed. A recent survey found that 71 per cent of respondents stated that their

organisation *expects* managerial support as part of the learning process.[24] Yet when asked what managers are expected to do, 63 per cent stated that managers are merely required to formally endorse the programme, and only 23 per cent required managers to *do* something, such as hold pre- and post-training discussions.

5. *Technical, commercial and operational considerations.* The proposal should contain all these elements: technical, covering whether and how the learning need can be addressed; commercial, containing an element of cost–benefit analysis; and operational, including a clear project plan with all the usual elements, such as budgets, resources, and quality and delivery gates. The proposal must also explicitly state the specific objectives and intended business impact of the learning solution. This may sound obvious, but it is important for three reasons: it is the mechanism through which you can ensure that the means and the ends of the learning are distinguishable and distinct; it sets the standards by which the programme can later be evaluated; and it sets the objectives behind which all other elements of the learning delivery operation can be aligned.

6. *Business-like presentation.* It is critical that the proposal reads like a commercial proposal because if it does not sound business-like, it will not be received as such. A key required skill here, then, is how to communicate technical issues without sounding too technical.

The completed proposal should provide absolute clarity on the business purpose of the solution, its achievability, the desired performance outcome, the broad design of the solution (e.g. training course, online learning or job aids), any challenges to be overcome and any risks to success that need to be mitigated. Only once you are armed with this should you decide whether to proceed or not, as it is only then that roles and responsibilities can be clarified and business sponsors' agreement on them be obtained. The final, agreed proposal can provide the basis for any outsourcing required and the criteria which any product development must meet. Indeed, it is only with a thorough proposal that functional alignment can be ensured in the product development stage: that you can be sure that the methods you use will be capable of delivering the desired results.

Assessing proposal making

Questions to ask yourself when reviewing a learning proposal

1. Have you involved key stakeholders in generating the proposal? Are you confident before the proposal is presented for decision-making that you garnered enough political support while it was being developed?
2. Does the proposal clearly state the objectives of the learning, in terms of both the targeted behaviour and how this will impact individual and organisational performance?
3. Is the identified learning issue genuinely a learning-related issue and an area in which it would be possible to deliver a significant improvement?
4. What would be the major risks to delivery, in terms of logistics and resources and the deliverability of a sustained performance increase?
5. How would the current business environment impact delivery and the application of learning to the workplace over a sustained period of time? What action would be required from the business to enable, encourage and support the required behaviour change?
6. Is the proposal sufficiently commercial in tone and does it contain all commercially relevant information? Is technical information presented in an expert yet business-friendly manner?

PRODUCT DEVELOPMENT

Now comes the third and final act, and with it the hard bit: designing and putting together a learning solution capable of achieving the behaviour change required. It is a complex task, and if it doesn't feel that way then it is a sure sign that something somewhere is being oversimplified. For starters, even setting aside how difficult behaviour change can be, there are a seemingly infinite number of variables involved, including those associated with the learning context, the learning content, the methods used, the media employed and the attributes and motivation of the learner. Unfortunately there are few if any hard and fast rules to guide us through this maze, as there is no evidence to show that any one method is always more effective than the rest, and what *is* effective changes according to the various combinations of variables associated with each situation.

Moreover, although new technologies can appear a boon, they are also for the moment a double-edged sword. More options may mean more opportunities, but they also mean more choice and therefore more difficult decisions in working out which is best for a particular situation. And as is often the case, research is lagging behind innovation, making it harder to know what is a passing fad and what really works.[25] For example, although a wide range of technologies and delivery methods can be used for blended learning,[26] little is known about the comparative effectiveness of specific blends. This makes it hard for practitioners to identify the best blend for their needs, an issue not made any less confusing by the tendency of providers to express their own opinions. Making a judicious choice is difficult, all the more so because heavy investments are often required. I return to this issue in Chapter 4, where I also explore some of the specific methods and tools that can be used.

For the moment I focus on what you need to do to ensure alignment between the methods and tools you use and the objectives you need to attain, although there is a relative paucity of advice on the matter. A Corporate Research Forum report concluded that the most important issue in product development was that solutions should be aligned with business and learning needs rather than with budgetary or political issues.[27] So far, so obvious. More specific factors that have been suggested as important include the characteristics of the content, the conditions in which an approach is undertaken, the resources available, and the target audience.[28] Perhaps we should not be too surprised at the lack of guidance, however, since given the sheer number of variables involved, any such list or attempt to match method with need risks being incomplete or oversimplistic.

Acknowledging this, Michael Connell, of the learning apps development company Native Brain, has recently approached the issue from the opposite direction, warning against two common product development strategies that should *not* be used. First, *following the herd*, using popularity or what other organisations are doing as a guide for what you should do. And second, *letting the customer decide*, using business and participant input and feedback as the main driver of design. Connell notes that although both of these crowdsourcing techniques can be useful components of a wider product development process, they have severe weaknesses when used in isolation,[29] and I would add that they betray a lack of expertise or confidence, or both, on the part of product developers.

A few general rules are, however, distinguishable and I suggest six key actions to ensure that the product created is capable of meeting the learning needs being targeted. These six recommendations are not a complete list of all that is important in product development, but each is critical in ensuring the functional alignment of the end solution with the required objectives.

1. *Fulfil the proposal.* The product development needs to be an extension of the proposal. This may sound obvious – and it is – but it is not uncommon for the proposal making and the product development to be undertaken by different people, sometimes in different organisations. It is important that all the strands and subtleties of the proposal are not lost and that the product development meets the criteria for successful delivery identified in the proposal.

2. *Be relevant, but don't overdo it.* The move towards learning objectives that more directly or obviously support organisational priorities has meant that the relevance of the learning content to learners' day-to-day work tasks has also become increasingly important. The easiest way to ensure relevance is by directly involving the business in designing learning solutions, most typically by using a small business-based group of subject matter experts. Yet there is a delicate juggling act required here because, left to their own devices, many business people tend to think in terms of learning methods that they know or like or feel comfortable with. So product developers need to balance this tendency with some expert insight. Some businesses choose to involve external experts for precisely this reason. I do not subscribe to the idea that an external perspective is always required, but having a clear plan for how you will achieve both relevance and a cutting edge is recommended.

3. *Be clear about how you will change behaviour.* One of the most frequently overlooked considerations during the development of learning solutions is an understanding of how people learn and change behaviour.[30] When it is present, it often does not go much beyond a fairly simplistic model of learning or thinking style. Yet the fact that individual learning style is usually the only factor considered can be viewed as a hangover from traditional, academic models of learning. Kolb's[31] and Honey and Mumford's[32] models of learning may be useful, but there is more to changing people's behaviour than mere learning style, and the expertise of corporate learning functions should extend beyond these models. This is not the correct forum to cover the various theories that try to explain how to change people's behaviour, but suffice to say that it should be a central issue and is one of the first questions we would ask of any solution provider: namely 'How do you understand that people learn and change behaviour and how does your proposed solution align with this?'

4. *Adapt to your audience.* As implied above, consideration of the targeted learning participants often does not extend much beyond learning style. With the growing use of single programmes across multiple locations, however, the consideration of target population characteristics has to become more sophisticated to take into account issues such as gender and generational and geographical differences.

5. *Tap into the learner's motivation.* Another, often overlooked, issue is the motivation of the learner,[33] and it is increasing in importance. Historically, the usually implicit assumption has been that by developing themselves, employees could either obtain better rewards or advance their careers. Indeed, in the 1990s 'enhancing your employability' was a byword for learning. Yet the link between learning and reward is not always direct or clear for employees to see, and there is little firm evidence that engaging in corporate learning enhances career progression.[34] Moreover, the immediate, inherent attractiveness of learning to employees is growing less obvious too, as it is increasingly linked to regulatory procedures and organisations are trying to align learning with business strategy more and more. So while the *why* of learning is probably being better articulated from the organisation's point of view than ever before, this seems to be at the expense of the *why* or *what's in it for me* from the individual's point of view. Any successful attempt at product development, therefore, must contain a clear plan for motivating and incentivising learners.

6. *Create a life-support system*. As I noted earlier, the workplace environment is often not ideal for learning. Failure is punished, there is a lack of time to reflect, and there is pressure to finish current tasks as quickly as possible.[35] Every learning solution produced must therefore contain a life-support system for the learning objective – some kind of a plan to help it survive and thrive in the day-to-day maelstrom of business life. And, as has previously been alluded to, this cannot simply amount to placing responsibility for this solely on line managers. One increasingly explored option, for instance, is to look at the potential beneficial impact of peers on the application of learning. The finished solution, then, must include a comprehensive plan for what happens after the primary learning event (e.g. the training day) is over and extends beyond the behaviour of line managers. We'll take a look at some of these options in Chapter 4.

Together, these six recommendations, although not sufficient to ensure alignment, will get most learning solutions a significant proportion of the way there. Though simplicity in solutions is always advisable, the process of developing solutions is rarely simple and, for me, a cause of instant suspicion. Product development is hard, and arguably harder now than it has ever been before. So if it seems easy, you are probably not doing it right.

Assessing product development

Questions to ask yourself when reviewing a new product

1. Does the process deliver to each and all of the objectives and criteria for success set out in the proposal?
2. Is the learning content and method both business-relevant and cutting edge (where appropriate)?
3. What is your theory of how to change behaviour? How does the developed process align with and fulfil these ideas? What are the potential consequences of your theory of behaviour change for the delivery of this learning solution and does the business share your understanding and expectations with regard to these issues?
4. Will the developed learning process be equally applicable and user-friendly for all members of the target audience or will it favour particular audience segments (e.g. particular learning styles, genders or generations)?

5.   Have you defined *'what's in for me?'* from the learner's perspective? How will the target audience be encouraged, motivated and/or incentivised to change behaviour in the desired way?

6.   How will the workplace environment help and/or hinder learning and behaviour change both immediately following the learning and over time? What is the likely 'decay' rate of the learning? What solutions to these issues have you included in the process and will they be sufficient?

CONCLUDING THOUGHTS

There is no doubt that, viewed from the end-user perspective, corporate learning solutions have made huge advances over the past decade or two. They certainly look and feel very different to those of twenty years ago. Yet for all the apparent progress, I believe that the movement is less substantial than it seems and that corporate learning in fact remains encumbered by many of its historical assumptions and traditions. In this chapter I have looked at changes – or the lack thereof – in the development of learning solutions. I have explored the underlying, but fundamental and persistent, influence of academic ways of thinking and talking about learning and how they can undermine our ability to functionally align the learning solutions that we develop with the learning outcomes that we need to produce. And I have shown how we need to rethink the process of developing solutions, introducing a more commercial, behavioural, contextual and longitudinal perspective.

There are those who argue that no matter how different corporate learning may look and feel, it will always remain the same content-driven, certification-based process it has always been. There is also a growing body of opinion that while this may be so, the future of learning development will be fundamentally different from its past, as new technologies enable not just new delivery methods but open up the use of new pedagogies – new ways of teaching.[36] I do not know if the future of learning *will* be any different from its past, but I firmly believe that it ought to be. Much of the progress perceived today is simply due to a sharpened focus on outputs and the appearance of new technologies, and if we are to successfully deliver these outputs and make the most of the new technologies available to us, then we need to start doing things that not only look different but also *are* different. And I look at how to achieve this in the next chapter, with the delivery of learning solutions.

4   Delivering learning solutions: technology and pedagogy explained

If the development of learning solutions has seen disappointingly little innovation over the past few decades, the delivery of them – the methods and media that we use to deliver and transmit what we want people to learn – is changing at a bewildering pace. Go to any learning conference, and the talk is all about a swathe of new technologies and the opportunities they offer: social networking, virtual worlds and serious games are the headline buzzwords of the day. Case studies showcasing the latest Next Big Thing seem to adorn every journal and magazine. And then there are the endless acronyms. CMS, LMS, KMS, LCMS, LKMS and – of course – LOKMS, MLE, PLE and VLE: the list goes on.* Many of them seem to mean the same thing, and some don't seem to mean much at all.

This confusion of terminologies reflects the state of development of learning technologies: it is still early days, in which options proliferate and the best ways forward are still unclear. This is partly why, despite all the talk and hype, organisations for the moment appear to remain cautious in the uptake of these new delivery methods.[37] 'We're just not ready' is the phrase I hear most often. Other reasons are that it feels too risky: many of the new learning technologies are not proven and the pace of change is so fast that an investment in a particular technology today may be superseded tomorrow. As we will see, these concerns are not unfounded. They also appear to be widespread, with one recent survey showing only

---

* Content Management System, Learning Management System, Knowledge Management System, Learning Content Management System, Learning Knowledge Management System, Learning Object Knowledge Management System, Managing Learning Environment, Personal Learning Environment and Virtual Learning Environment.

12 per cent of corporate learning respondents reporting a preference for innovation.[38] For the moment, then, tried and trusted methods remain the reality of learning delivery. Yet change *is* coming, and in a big way. Some of the new technologies will almost certainly turn out to be passing fads, but others are here to stay and they promise to bring with them nothing short of a complete reconceptualisation of how learning is delivered. For they hold the promise of changing not only how learning looks and feels but also what it can do.[39] The times, to borrow from the Bob Dylan song, really do seem to be a-changin'.

WHY IS THE LEARNING DELIVERY LANDSCAPE CHANGING?

This chapter is about the coming change, the new wave of technologies, and how the learning delivery landscape is transforming with their arrival. Let's begin, though, by taking a brief step back to look at *why* things are changing – at the forces at play that provide the context for all the change we are currently seeing. Five forces of change, in particular, stand out (see Figure 4.1).

Increasingly distributed and diverse workforces

Globalisation is nothing new, but it is reaching new heights and having a fundamental impact on learning delivery. In fact, it is probably the most common reason we encounter for organisations seeking to use online learning. As workforces become more distributed, organisations are having to find new and better ways to replicate or scale up their learning programmes across geographies,[40] often in the face of variable HR infrastructure and differing legal environments. This is sometimes driven by a need for consistency, sometimes by a push for greater cost-effectiveness, and sometimes by a desire to transfer 'home' practices to foreign operations. Virtual working is also leading organisations to explore new technologies that enable employees to access learning and performance support tools remotely. Moreover, with these distribution needs have come diversity needs, as teams

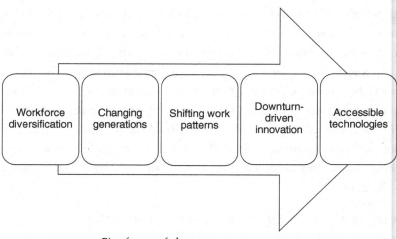

FIGURE 4.1 Five forces of change

increasingly comprise employees from multiple countries. This is not a new issue, but it is changing significantly. A few years ago the focus was on adapting learning content to meet local cultural needs. Today, in the face of new research showing that cultural differences exist in receptivity to and participation rates in different delivery methods,[41] corporate learning functions are increasingly having to look at adapting how they deliver this content as well.

Generational change in the workforce

The workforce is changing in other ways too. The post-war Baby Boomer generation is reaching retirement age and in just a few years' time, nearly half the workforce will be made up of those who were born after 1980. Whether you call them Gen Y, Millennials, Echo Boomers, First Digitals or the iGeneration, their arrival is heralding big changes in corporate learning. Like every new generation, they have different learning preferences, different expectations of work, and they use new technologies more. Yet there is growing evidence that the expectations and needs of this next generation may well prove so different as to require significant changes in corporate learning.

Most fundamentally, members of this next generation do not merely use new technologies more, they use them differently. They are used to having immediate access to information anywhere anytime, take for granted the collaborative nature of wikis and knowledge sharing, and expect to be able to connect with others using online social networking. These differences are driving different expectations of learning, such as that it should be ongoing and immediately accessible. Some of these differences are less obvious, too: for example, despite all the stereotypes about technology making them less prone to personal interaction, there is evidence that this generation may be more socially connected than their predecessors[42] and that they may tend to show a greater preference for face-to-face learning.[43] Juggling the expectations and needs of different generations has never been harder and it is leading organisations to consider new ways of delivering learning.

The changing nature of work

It is not just the workforce that is changing: the workplace is, too. Business cycles in many industries are shortening, with new products emerging every six to nine months. More generally, busy chief executives, under pressure to transform their organisations within two or three years, don't have time for gradual change and need instead to cascade new strategies, behaviour or culture across geographies and time zones within short periods of time. This requires more rapid deployment of learning support, and new technologies are seen as a solution.

Moreover, a new enemy of productivity is emerging in the form of time constraints, and learning delivery has become one of the frontlines of this battle. Leaner, more dynamic and faster-paced work environments leave little time for learning and guarantee distracted learners. Putting work on hold for a training course is a luxury that many workers cannot afford any more. A recent survey found that 40 per cent of those who refused training that was offered did so because they felt they were too busy.[44] Preference for shorter training time is repeatedly being reported, too, with learners now opting for two-day courses, rather than the week-long programmes of the past, and online learning slots of thirty to sixty minutes.[45] The exemplar here is the Khan Academy – a non-profit educational organisation that provides a free online collection of more than 3,000 micro lectures, lasting only four to fifteen minutes – and many organisations and providers are seeking to replicate this approach with bite-sized learning nuggets.

Downturn-driven innovation

It has been said that there is nothing like a war to drive innovation. The same can be said of an economic downturn. Faced with tight budgets, corporate learning functions are trying to find new ways to do more with less. Centralisation, streamlining and outsourcing are all providing opportunities to realise efficiencies, and online learning and internal knowledge-sharing are both on the increase and delivering cost savings.[46] Yet whereas previous downturns tended to create a simple focus on cost control, this time around the focus has also been on demonstrating value and ensuring quality and consistency.

Many of the changes we are seeing in this vein began before the downturn, but the recent economic conditions have increased the pace of change and the presence of technology-facilitated delivery channels is enabling organisations to focus on innovation and not just efficiency. The reaction to reduced travel budgets is a good example: ten years ago this would have signalled a reduction in learning activity; this time organisations seem more focused on creating and using geography-crossing delivery methods.[47]

The spread of cost-effective, accessible technologies

The meeting point of the above four drivers of change and, to a large extent, also the solution for each is technology. In itself, learning technology is nothing new. The behavioural psychologist B.F. Skinner was exploring the use of automated learning using mechanical devices over fifty years ago. And mobile phones and the Internet, the foundations of modern learning technologies, have been around for many years. Indeed, in many ways what we are witnessing now is a second coming of learning technology.

The first wave came in the millennial years, when a whole raft of e-learning companies quickly opened and just as quickly closed as they found out the hard way that the technology infrastructure was not developed enough to support them (e.g. lack of cheap broadband access). Four things are different now. First, the technology is better, with massive improvements in bandwidth, people now carrying powerful computers in their pockets and integration between devices that seemed very separate ten years ago. Second, the rate of technology product innovation is accelerating, with open source development and the 'appification' of software (the move to smaller, more specific applications) together speeding the route to implementation. Third, these technologies have now become sufficiently commoditised to be cost-effective to use. And fourth, access to these technologies has reached a critical mass. Widespread availability of unlimited data plans drove mobile media in Japan and this is now driving the same expansion in the United States and Europe. The latest figures show six billion cellular phone contracts worldwide – equivalent to 86 per cent of the world population. Over 85 per cent of new mobile handsets are web-enabled, an estimated 55 million web-enabled tablets were sold in 2011 alone, and by 2016, one billion people will own smartphones, many of whom will be professionals taking these devices to work.

The technological infrastructure necessary for online learning is thus firmly established and the majority of medium-sized and large corporations and universities have extensive IT divisions to manage and develop their systems. So it is not so much an era of technology, but of accessible, mobile, cost-effective technology. We have reached a tipping point at which technology has become sufficiently cheap and networks have become sufficiently fast, which is finally enabling genuinely new technologies to emerge.

THE COMING CHANGE

Together these forces of change are creating a perfect storm: a collision of downturn-driven innovation, maturing technology infrastructure, and changing workforces and workplaces. So what are the changes we are seeing? What exactly is all the hype about?

The headline acts are easy to spot. Augmented reality (AR) is one of the big buzzwords – the blend of real views of physical environments with virtual reality. Some much-vaunted applications of this technology have recently launched: for example, BMW and Volkswagen use it to train service personnel in the maintenance and repair of their new vehicle models. Virtual worlds such as Second Life have also had their day in the sun, and although they capture fewer headlines today than they did a few years ago, they continue to capture the imagination as venues for real-time learning events and simulations. And serious games, 'funware' and 'edutainment' are also attracting attention, with research coming out of higher education showing that students in classes using games do better than students in classes not using games.[48]

These interesting and exciting-sounding attention grabbers are hard to miss and promise much. A virtual revolution, as their promoters would say: they are the future and it is bright. Yet for all the promise and possibilities, I find myself disagreeing. Because for me, the real change and the real revolution lie elsewhere, under the surface and hidden from view behind these new technologies. To help show this, let's take a look at two of the most discussed technological developments of the past ten years: e-learning and m-learning, or mobile learning.

HOW WE GOT HERE: FROM E-LEARNING TO M-LEARNING

If it feels as if we've been here before, we have. Ten years ago many were convinced that we were entering a golden age of technology-enhanced learning, or e-learning. In one of the most famous statements on the subject, John Chambers, CEO of Cisco, said, 'Education over the internet is going to be so big it is going to make email usage look like a rounding error.' Fortunately for him, he didn't promise to eat his hat if it didn't happen.

The millennial e-learning wave involved the emergence of two main technologies: Learning Content Management Systems (LCMSs) for storing and providing learning materials online; and Learning Management Systems (LMSs) for managing course communications and logistics using specially designed software. The fact that these systems did not deliver on all the hope and hype was undoubtedly in part due to the immaturity of the technology, but it was also due to *how* businesses and educational institutions started using them. In the initial haste towards implementation, existing learning content was often just transferred into online databases, and more than a few organisations saw these systems purely as an opportunity to cut costs by replacing traditional face-to-face learning with e-learning.

Many organisations failed to appreciate that distance e-learning, no matter how dressed up it is in shiny technological clothes, is a poor replacement for face-to-face learning. With the clarity of hindsight, the result was inevitable. Surveys started reporting that many employees preferred face-to-face programmes,[49] were less engaged by online courses,[50] and that high dropout rates were commonplace.[51] Disappointment and disillusionment set in.

Things are slowly improving. The social element has been reintroduced by providing a blend of both e-learning and traditional classroom learning, and there is a growing emphasis on usability. The first systems were predominantly designed for the benefit of the organisation, and this showed in their front-end user experience. Ten years on, however, the iPhone generation has much higher expectations of usability, and providers are stepping up to meet this challenge with newer, simpler system interfaces. The most significant development, though, is that organisations are finally beginning to use these systems to make learning happen in different ways.

For example, collaboration is emerging. This was always a key part of most LCMSs, enabling learning designers to collaborate online to develop content. What is new now is that systems are allowing learners to interact and collaborate through wikis, blogs and 'communities of practice' (more on these later). This is significant because it effectively promises to solve a problem that has historically been the Achilles heel of all distance learning and generally thought to be unavoidable: namely, that it occurs at a distance. With the advent of webinars, web-based video conferencing and live streaming, employees across the globe can now attend the same learning events at the same time, and the use of instant messaging and live chat allows them to interact and be active participants as they do so. These new technologies are thus transforming how learning happens at a distance, increasing learner connectivity and decreasing dropout rates in the process.

There is another change, too. You'll notice it in the way providers talk about their systems: mention of compliance tracking is for the most part gone, replaced by talk of how LMSs can function as portals to Virtual Learning Environments (VLEs). Some of this language is about hyping up products, but it also reflects how people are thinking more about the impact of technology on the process and experience of learning. This gives me hope that these systems may finally deliver on their promise of revolution by enabling us not only to spread the learning content around further but also to do something different with it.

If e-learning opened up access, taking learning out of the classroom, mobile learning, or m-learning, is extending the concept and taking it away from any fixed point.[52] It promises to fuel an age of 'anytime anywhere' learning. Just as the development of e-learning was built on the back of existing technology (the Internet), m-learning is seeking to use existing trends. Today 85 per cent of companies provide mobile devices to some of their employees[53] and mobile devices already account for 10 per cent of all website hits. Love it or loathe it, mobile technology is here to stay and it will continue to make inroads into everyday life. This is why most commentators now see the rise of m-learning as inevitable.

M-learning is still at an embryonic stage and, as in the early days of e-learning, it has so far predominantly been used as a simple distribution tool – delivering the same old learning via new media. And for this purpose it can, indeed, be useful. It is being used to support learners who do not have immediate access to computers, such as retail clerks and sales people, and anyone working on the move. There are reports of schools using iPads for homework; Apple's iTunes University has ensured that thousands of podcasts and videos of lectures are now freely available on the move; and medical schools, corporate universities and companies are all using mobile technology to improve access to learning resources.[54]

However, I believe that although accessibility on the go is a powerful development that could have broad societal impact, for corporate learning functions the true promise of the technology lies not in its ability to help us do things more widely or more cheaply but in its ability to enable us to do things differently. At IMD, for example – one of the top ranked business schools in the world – executive development programme participants receive iPads with a specially designed application that enables them to access all course materials and to interact with these materials and exchange thoughts with other participants and faculty via a preloaded iPad address book with dedicated email addresses. So IMD is using m-learning not only to make access to learning easier and more convenient (no more heavy folders with printed presentations and case studies) but also to increase collaborative learning opportunities.

Another example of m-learning opening up new opportunities is 'just-in-time learning': specific pieces of information being delivered when and where they are needed. A great example of this can be found in institutions such as museums that are using the location-aware abilities of smartphones to provide augmented reality learning aids.[55] Just point your phone at an object, and it will tell you all about the artefact. Similarly, hospitals are now encouraging the use of mobile technology to provide newly qualified doctors with information on demand. This kind of learning is being called direct performance support, and to a time-poor generation it can sound like the Promised Land, delivering tailored, specific learning nuggets about what you want to know, when you most need to know it.

Mobile technology is also being used to transform traditional learning methods such as lectures with 'backchannelling'. Several years ago, audience members at presentations and workshops began communicating with one another via Twitter and social networking sites using their smartphones and laptops. Seeing the power of this, conferences and workshops are now setting up official backchannels,[56] which allow delegates to tweet brief comments and questions in response to the speakers and the comments of other tweeters, and there are even reports of conferences projecting Twitter posts on a screen behind the speaker.[57] This sounds like hell for speakers and faculty members such as myself, but it opens up an amazing new way of enabling a more engaging, interactive and collaborative type of learning. Just as with e-learning, m-learning technology can be used to improve access, as well as to change how learning happens. And it is in this kind of change that the real revolution lies.

EVOLUTION AND REVOLUTION

For all their novelty, the new technologies we see emerging today can in many ways be seen as simple evolutions of age-old learning methods. Funware may sound as modern as it gets, but using games for learning is nothing new, and the first computer games designed for learning appeared back in the 1970s. Likewise, the online distribution of learning materials is not really that much different from the use of radio and television for education. There are thus those who argue that, for all the glitter and glamour of new technologies, corporate learning is still much the same as it was during the Industrial Age of the nineteenth century. There is, they say, no revolution.

The frustration and passion for me is that there could be, should be and needs to be some revolution. We are at a critical intersection in the development of learning technologies and we see two paths ahead. Down one road, corporate learning functions could continue to experiment with new technologies, gradually using them more and more, but not fundamentally change how they approach learning delivery. The result would be some success, improved user experience and some reasonably good outcomes and feedback. This sounds okay, as results go. Yet down the other path, we have the opportunity to use these new technological tools to fundamentally change learning delivery with new ways of teaching and learning. And we need to do something radical if we are to deliver real and long overdue improvement in the persistently poor outcomes associated with the transfer of training and also in the generally miserable satisfaction ratings that corporate learning functions tend to receive.

In the initial rush first to e-learning and now to m-learning there has been too much focus on the technology and not enough on how it is being used. As a result, there is a real risk that much of the potential of these new technologies will not be realised. The challenge for corporate learning functions is to look beyond the shiny and exciting new technologies arrayed before them, and to start seeing them not as learning solutions in themselves but as tools and enablers of learning. They need to stop thinking about the technology and start thinking about the pedagogy that underpins it.

THE IMPORTANCE OF BEING PEDAGOGICAL

Ten years ago the main barriers to the successful use of learning technologies were technological. Today they are pedagogical – with how technologies are being used.[58] Commentator after commentator is reporting that educational and corporate learning professionals' lack of familiarity with technology and how to use it is a fundamental barrier to success, and a study from the US-based National Center for Education Statistics has concurred, noting that one of the greatest challenges of teaching online is the lack of guidance on exactly how to do so.

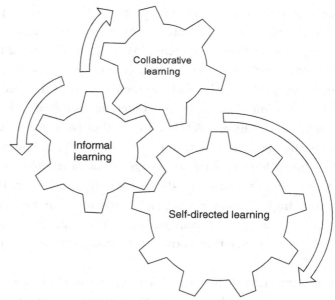

FIGURE 4.2 Three technology-enabled pedagogies

There is, unfortunately, no single, agreed list of different pedagogies that can be referred to. However, looking at the new ways of learning that technologies are enabling, three pedagogies do stand out. They are not entirely separate, in that a single learning method is often a mix of two or more pedagogies, but each is distinct in its intent and impact. They are: collaborative learning, informal learning and self-directed learning (see Figure 4.2).

Collaborative learning

If you post on Pinterest, a pinboard-style content sharing website, or have contributed to Wikipedia, then you are already acquainted with collaborative learning. It is also one of the most talked about trends in corporate learning. It involves using web-based technologies to create forums – called Collaborative Learning Environments (CLEs) – in which ideas, knowledge and expertise can be exchanged and jointly developed. Twenty years ago this would have necessitated getting people together in the same room or on a conference call. These days, employees thousands of miles apart can access and contribute to CLEs from any web-connected device, be it their tablet, phone or television.

Probably the most common corporate use of these tools is in 'communities of practice': websites where employees can go to share ideas, ask questions and collaborate on projects. These collaborative communities vary in size and sophistication. They include everything from the simple use of email or websites to share documents, raise and answer questions, and exchange ideas to combinations of synchronous and asynchronous tools to help participants create ideas. Asynchronous learning is similar to traditional distance learning in that it involves participants accessing course materials independently and at different times; synchronous learning involves participants learning the same things at the same times. This used to mean being in the same place, too, though not any more.

The use of synchronous and asynchronous tools in collaborative learning is sometimes referred to as Web 2.0 – the use of online spaces to allow users to interact with one another as creators of content. By allowing users to actively engage and share knowledge with one another, corporate learning functions are not only enabling and encouraging employees to teach one another but are also actively fostering the types of conversations that lead to creativity and problem solving. Organisations are thus using communities of practice as knowledge-management tools and to drive innovation, in particular in technical disciplines.

As a pedagogy, collaborative learning enables more engaging and immersive learning and provides just-in-time access to information. Indeed, although the use of collaborative tools to enable innovation is currently grabbing all the headlines, it is the knowledge management function that may well prove to have more impact for businesses. Ensuring knowledge transfer across siloed business structures is one of the biggest learning challenges facing organisations today, and for many it is easier to find a long-lost high school friend on the other side of the world than it is to find out a piece of work-related information from the other side of the business. Collaborative organisation-centric social network tools have the potential to solve this issue, and along these lines, some companies are using such tools to better connect the about-to-retire Baby Boomer generation with their successors, in an attempt to ensure that their experience and expertise are not lost.

Yet just because these new technologies exist does not mean that they will be effectively used. It is still early days for technology-enabled collaborative learning, and how to determine the right mix of components for particular contexts is only beginning to be researched. Some issues are already clear, though. For example, the most effective collaborative tools are those that involve the continued involvement of facilitators and instructors. In addition, a sizeable minority of employees may need training in online communication skills before they can make the most of being involved in CLEs. So a strong understanding of what collaborative learning is, can do and requires in order to be effective is essential if corporate learning functions are to make the most of this promising and popular pedagogy.

Informal learning

If there is one pedagogy that can beat collaborative learning to the top of most commentators' 'top trends' lists it is informal learning. A recent survey found that 25 per cent of US companies invested in informal learning in 2011 and that their average spend was double what it was in 2010.[59] Unlike formal learning, which refers to organised instructional activities, informal learning is spontaneous and self-initiated and does not follow a pre-planned curriculum or occur in a specified place.[60] Examples of informal learning include sharing resources with others, searching the Internet for information, and experimenting with new techniques or tools. Three types of informal learning are often distinguished: *on-demand* methods, such as articles, podcasts and performance support tools; *social* methods, such as coaching, wikis and communities of practice; and *embedded* methods, such as feedback, after-event reviews and development planning.

The reason for the growing popularity of these methods is that they are often seen as mimicking 'natural' learning – how people learn outside work and educational environments. Research suggests that regardless of the amount of training provided to employees, the majority of their learning occurs through natural, day-to-day learning processes, often in the form of consultation and collaboration within the immediate working group. Indeed, the combination of this perceived efficiency and the cost savings inherent in these methods compared with formal learning offerings has ensured that they have quickly become one of the most desired approaches available.

New technologies are transforming informal learning in two ways. First, they are vastly increasing access to information. And second, they are enabling the formalisation of informal learning by providing structured learning environments in which learners can engage in it. With this in mind, many LMS providers are now incorporating tools such as moderated chat rooms in their system design and focusing on enabling on-demand, just-in-time access to the right information at the right time.

Yet a lack of understanding about what informal learning is and how it works is causing some organisations to miss out on its full potential. For example, I have observed some organisations that appear to mistakenly believe that merely establishing a solution for internal wikis or blogs means they have an informal learning strategy. Effective informal learning is not about enabling knowledge sharing per se, but about enabling the right knowledge to be shared and accessible. And any search engine provider can confirm that this is no easy feat. Filtering content to avoid overwhelming users with information is fast becoming a key challenge, and 'knowledge curation' – the task of ensuring that only the best, authoritative and current content is made available – is becoming an industry in its own right. Moreover, effective informal learning in corporate environments needs to mimic the process of 'natural' learning, as well as feeding into and fuelling individuals' natural desire to learn. Usability is thus becoming a key issue and heavy front-end testing of systems is on the increase. Thus, the promise of informal learning will only be fulfilled with careful consideration of the learning processes underpinning the myriad technologies and solutions that exist.

Self-directed learning

The third and final pedagogy to highlight is self-directed learning. It is an element inherent in most forms of collaborative and informal learning, and so is often wrongly assumed to be part of them. Sometimes referred to as 'learner-centred', self-directed learning enables learners to decide what, where and when they will learn. It is more than offering learning content through different media to accommodate personal preferences or allowing users to change the font size and background colour; it places control of learning itself into the hands of the learners. Technology enables this by providing Personal Learning Environments (PLEs): customisable portals to learning content that employ filtering technologies to recognise individual users and their preferences and provide them with highly personalised experiences. Many see these systems as the next generation of learning management, and research is showing that their use can result in increased engagement and motivation.

At a time when organisational learning needs are receiving more attention, it may at first seem strange to discover that recent surveys show that the top tools in use are predominantly used to deliver self-paced content, tailored to individual needs.[61] Yet, far from being at odds with organisational objectives, self-directed learning can even reinforce them. For example, PLEs are not incompatible with curriculums and instead provide a means for corporate learning functions to endorse learner preferences while also providing relevant and useful content. In this way, modern technology-enabled self-directed learning methods hold the promise of at least partly resolving the age-old tension between providing learning to large groups and allowing for individual differences.

As with the other pedagogies I have highlighted, though, the fulfilment of this promise will depend upon careful application. There are some areas, for example, in which the use of self-directed learning is not appropriate or perhaps even ethical, such as safety-related training. And businesses with a strong organisational development agenda may need to think twice about whether they wish to hand over control. In addition, learner control may be provided along a number of dimensions, such as content, sequence or pace, and initial research is beginning to show that these dimensions may differ in their impact on the efficacy of learning.[62] Moreover, while some have highlighted the benefits of self-directed learning for time management, research is also showing the importance of ensuring learners have these time management skills to begin with. Taking your horse to water is one thing; getting it to drink is quite another.

Case study: learning to be safe at BP

Ensuring the safety of workers in high-hazard conditions is a challenging task. The primary role of learning teams in these environments is to provide workers with the knowledge and skills they require to remain safe. Yet this kind of training can only do so much. To ensure safety as far as is possible, learning teams also need to find ways of promoting a 'safety culture': an environment that keeps safety at the forefront of people's thinking and supports the identification of risks.

An interesting recent example of such a safety culture programme is BP's ToughTalk. Urbain Bruyere, VP Culture, Competency and Capability for the Group Safety & Operational Risk team, is the leader behind this initiative. The primary target audience is staff working in high-hazard operations such as refineries, chemical sites and offshore rigs. The most obvious challenge Urbain faced initially was a logistical one: how to deliver the learning product to a distributed audience, many of whom worked in remote locations.

The first draft of the programme, preoccupied with this distribution issue, was primarily a technological solution in that it used technology to deliver a basic learning product. Yet Urbain realised something was missing: the issue was not only distribution but also how to embed learning in the workplace to make it more than just a piece of information that was presented to learners. He also needed to work out how to truly engage learners who were time-poor and who had received a lot of previous training. So the development of the programme shifted from being a logistical issue with a technological solution to a learning issue about how to embed and engage learning, which demanded a pedagogical solution.

The solution that Urbain and his team developed was a classic mix of traditional pedagogies delivered through new technologies. To engage and embed the learning, they used two devices. First, they presented the learning not as facts but through storytelling, working with subject matter experts to develop a screenplay based on a selection of common behaviours and actions that had previously led to accidents. The screenplay was then developed by a professional film production company and turned into an 18-minute film, shot with a professional crew, on location. The result was a slick, realistically gritty and engaging portrayal of events. The film was distributed online and via DVDs. But that was the easy part, because Urbain was clear that the film itself was not a 'piece' of learning, just a stimulus for it.

So Urbain and his team developed a toolkit to help engage line managers in delivering the training to their teams. The film was cut down into a series of shorter mini-films, designed to be shown in the regular team meetings, and managers were provided with detailed guides on how to facilitate brief discussion sessions. During these sessions, learners are expected to work together to recognise particular dangers (e.g. declining standards or pressure to produce), discuss the potential for these dangers occurring at their site, and to come up with improvement actions that can immediately be put into practice. So although online storytelling may sound rather ethereal, Urbain and his team did not allow themselves to be dazzled by technology and instead focused on pedagogy – on how learners could learn. This allowed them to develop a highly practical and grounded solution capable of producing real safety improvements that can be shared across sites and which, as a bonus, also supports and promotes managers as developers of their people. After successful piloting, the programme launched across the business in the second half of 2012 and has received a cross-industry award.

USING PEDAGOGIES TO MAKE THE MOST OF TECHNOLOGY

My core belief is that when applying learning technologies, corporate learning functions need to understand, consider and think in terms of pedagogies such as these. They need to balance their current tendency to focus on *what* content and technology is being offered with an equal focus on *how* it is being offered and how it will or will not work. This may sound obvious, but historically speaking, organisations have tended to focus more on getting the content right than the teaching methods they are using. Yet with the sudden proliferation of technology-based tools, choosing the right method has never been more difficult or more important. Let us now consider three very basic questions that all organisations should ask when considering which pedagogy to use: which method or tool is best? How do we blend learning methods most effectively? And how do we ensure employees engage with and make the most of the learning offered?

Question 1: which method or tool is best?

This question is usually limited by the addition of the condition 'for my needs', which you would think would make the answer a lot easier. Unfortunately, it doesn't. A quick browse of Google reveals a lot of claims being made about the efficacy of various new technology-enabled delivery methods, and a lot of predictions about how this or that technology will become ubiquitous and essential. Yet, as so often happens, innovation is ahead of research. Many of these claims and predictions are being written by vested interests and there is a dearth of independent studies for learning professionals to consult. Moreover, many of the studies that do exist seem to be either one-off case studies or research conducted on university students, and there is a real shortage of good quality quantitative studies conducted in corporate settings. Furthermore, from the research that has been done, no single pedagogy has been shown to be inherently better than any other – a finding that is commonly referred to as the 'no-significant-difference phenomenon'.[63] So as yet, there is no clear answer to the 'which is best' question.

The impact of this lack of assurance is that companies are either holding back from using new technologies or are simply proceeding without really knowing if their investment will work. Consider this: in 2006, an incredible $125 million was spent on game-based learning without a body of independent research showing that it works in corporate learning.[64] I therefore suspect that, in the absence of real data, the choice of delivery mode is being driven less by a considered view of what works best and more by budgetary pressures, travel limitations and fads. For example, take the move towards bite-sized learning nuggets, such as Hemsley Fraser's 'Espresso Learning', TMI's 'Take 90s' or the work of the hugely successful company Mind Gym, which offers brief, specific 90-minute 'mental workouts'. These types of products are proving popular and generally receive plaudits and positive customer reactions. But as a number of commentators have recently noted, this popularity is juxtaposed by the fact that there is little research beyond customer reactions, so it is not yet clear if this type of bite-sized learning is an effective method for delivering sustained behaviour change and performance improvements.

This is where an understanding of pedagogies can prove essential. Without consensus on which tools or technology solutions to use in which situations, the best approach is for organisations to think of which teaching method is most able to produce the desired outcomes. As a starting point, ask yourself the following five questions:

1. How distributed are your learners? For example, if you need to deliver training on a new HR system across a global population, then an understanding of the challenges of distance learning will help you identify criteria for selecting which technology-enabled delivery solution to use.
2. How specific is the learning content? The less specific or the broader it is, the more room there is to employ self-directed learning techniques.
3. How critical is the learning objective? If you need to ensure that a series of legally required training content is undertaken, then formal learning is likely to be required and self-directed learning should only be used with care.
4. What preference does your audience have? For instance, research has shown that IT professionals prefer Internet searching, whereas HR professionals and public school teachers favour more interactive face-to-face activities.[65] As a note of caution, though, research has also repeatedly shown that what CLOs think their audience prefers more often than not does not tally with what their audience really wants.
5. To what degree is the learning objective about creating a cultural change? If it is cultural in nature, then collaborative and informal pedagogies will need to be central to what you do.

One noteworthy exception to the no-significant-difference phenomenon is that some researchers have suggested that although no single instructional method may be uniquely advantageous, using a variety of methods may be superior.[66] The idea here is simply that you are more likely to be effective using a broader range of methods since you have a better chance of connecting with your audience and because multiple methods – if combined well – will reinforce one another. While this is open to debate, research is showing that mixed method or 'blended' distance courses tend to result in better outcomes than traditional distance learning or face-to-face instruction alone.[67] And it is research such as this that has helped the rise of one of the most talked about approaches to learning delivery of recent years: blended learning.

Question 2: how do we blend learning most effectively?

As described in Chapter 3, blended learning is an approach to learning delivery that involves the use of multiple pedagogies. In its proper form, it is not a menu of options or a simple combination of different media, but an integrated offering in which learning is delivered through the use of different pedagogies. For example, someone might listen to a podcast (distance learning), then participate in a live-streamed video-based discussion group (collaborative distance learning), before joining a community of practice discussion (self-directed, collaborative learning), and finally use a mobile PLE to access reminders of how best to apply the learning (self-directed, informal distance learning). With the explosion of technology-driven non-traditional learning methods, blending is fast emerging as *the* design approach in corporate learning.

There are many forms of blending,[68] and deciding which to use is not easy. The most common form to date is the simple combining of online distance learning with traditional classroom learning.[69] Other examples include so-called anchor blends and bookend blends. In anchor blends, learning is begun (i.e. anchored) using familiar learning methods, and a less familiar teaching method is used afterwards. IBM, for example, has used a reverse anchor blend in its management training in which learners move from online and computer-based experiences to increasingly human and live ones.[70] In bookend blends, meanwhile, one type of learning occurs both before and after another form of learning. Cisco, for example, has adopted a bookend approach in which learners go through online course materials before they come to a classroom for face-to-face activities, and then return online for follow-up materials.[71]

The list of potential blending designs is almost endless and research is still to shed light on which types of blends are most suitable for which situations. So where do you begin? A common approach is for organisations, having opted for a blended solution, to choose their blend based on their preferred methods: a bit of trad-itional classroom (because the audience likes that), plus a bit of what provider A does (because we like what they do), and then a bit of follow-on coaching or e-learning, all wrapped up in an attractive technological package. However, something is missing: the element of integration and consideration of how the various pedagogies will interact with and impact one another. A delicate balancing act is required to get blended learning right, and simply throwing every-thing into a pot is unlikely to yield the maximum potential of each of the individual ingredients.

To ensure this happens, I recommend a simple, four-step recipe.

1. Divide your overall learning objectives into smaller learning chunks. They should be specific and clear about how behaviour will change as a result, and how this will in turn impact performance.
2. For each individual objective, look at which pedagogy is most likely to deliver the behaviour changes and performance improvements required.
3. Only once the pedagogies have been identified should you explore the options for delivery solutions (e.g. which technologies to use).
4. Consider carefully how each of the different learning blocks, pedagogies and delivery solutions can be woven into a cohesive and integrated learning experience.

Question 3: how do we ensure employees engage with the learning offered?

Revolution rarely comes without challenge. The key challenges that organisations are reporting in the deployment of new pedagogically driven blended learning solutions are not financial or technological, as might be expected. Instead, top of the list come lack of expertise, difficulty in harnessing the support of line managers for new ways of learning, and lack of skills and motivation among employees to manage and drive their own learning.[72] Of these, the single most reported issue is undoubtedly the matter of motivation.

Motivation has long been identified as vital to successful learning, but it is increasingly coming under the spotlight as organisations have started using learning methodologies that rely more on learners' willingness to actively invest time and effort in the learning process. For example, I have come across many communities of practice and collaborative Web 2.0 tools that are not gaining traction with today's time-poor employees because they are seen as something extra to do. And when a voluntary option is seen as taking time away from what is most important, it simply will not be chosen. The rejection of learning offerings is not always immediate or obvious. There are a growing number of case studies highlighting how employees have initially expressed great enthusiasm toward online learning systems only to later stop using them almost completely, presumably as the novelty wears off and the time pressures of day-to-day business life come to bear.[73] The rejection does not always involve complete withdrawal from learning, though, as studies have shown, disengaged learners can also sometimes satisfy only the minimum requirements of involvement. They can thus appear to be involved, while not really being so.

Some commentators have responded by suggesting that where employee motivation is particularly important for learning outcomes, more unencumbered time needs to be built into employees' work days.[74] But in my view this is not a politically realistic option in many businesses and there is no guarantee that learners will fill this unencumbered time with actual learning. Another response has been to suggest simply using more engaging methodologies, with self-directed learning, collaborative learning and game-based learning all being touted as solutions. Yet this feels like avoiding the issue and we cannot assume that these methodologies *are* more engaging for all learners. The most promising response, however, is to use 'scaffolding'.

Scaffolding is the deliberate, structured and planned use of activities outside the core delivery of learning that support the process of learning and the transfer of this learning into behaviour change and performance improvement. The range of techniques used is considerable and includes:

- Training and other support given to line managers to help them support their employees' learning.
- The use of reflective peer-to-peer blogging.
- Testing (following research showing that students who are tested show better recall of learning than those who are not).
- The use of 'reflection triggers', such as follow-on emails asking questions about learning content.
- The use of text messaging to conduct and then communicate the results of spot polls.

Research on the efficacy of many of these is still lacking. For example, it has been suggested that although reflection triggers appear to be appreciated by learners and favoured by learning professionals, they do not necessarily help produce increased performance.[75] One area where research has shown that there is much to be gained, however, and which promises to become a core required skill for learning professionals, is 'gameification'. This is not the inclusion of games, but the use of gameplay mechanics for non-game applications. These mechanics are the techniques and mechanisms used to encourage users to play games and generally involve measuring progress, providing feedback and rewarding effort and success.

Examples of these techniques include point systems, achievement badges, progress bars, and tangible rewards and incentives. Good exemplars of this are the achievement levelling used in Six Sigma training (are you a black belt yet?) and the use of puzzles and levels by Rosetta Stone to motivate their language learners. A further example of gameification is the structuring of learning into 'layers'. Games are often structured to have the long-term goal of completing the game, the medium-term goal of completing levels in the game, and the short-term goal of completing missions in the levels. Similarly, when designing e-learning material, developers can break up content into short-term, medium-term and long-term goals.

The significance of the arrival of scaffolding and gameification methods should not be underestimated. They are an important part of the learning revolution, since they lead us to consider how people learn and the pedagogies that we are using. But they do something else, as well. They remind us that – deep down – learning in a corporate context is not so much about knowledge acquisition as about behaviour change and performance improvement. Though dressed in modern language, gameification and scaffolding are founded on a century of research into the psychology of behaviour and methods of behaviour change. Importantly, unexpectedly and on the quiet, these techniques promise to rectify the current absence of behaviour change theory in corporate learning, which I believe is at the heart of our persistent inability to improve our hit rate in delivering learning that is transferred into the workplace. In Chapter 3 I lamented the fact that corporate learning seems at times to be almost divorced from the subject of behaviour change. Here, beneath all the glamour and hype of technology-enabled solutions, lies the promise that this critical missing link will be reconnected.

Learning delivery audit

Questions you need to be able to answer to be sure that you are using learning technologies effectively

1. Which and how many learning technologies are currently in use across your organisation? What proportion of your learning is delivered via technology-enabled means?
2. How much do they cost and what evidence do you have of their impact?
3. Have learning technologies historically been introduced more for logistical reasons (enabling access) or for pedagogical reasons?
4. How are learning technologies being used in your organisation – what kinds of learning pedagogies do they enable?
5. Which pedagogies do you use? To what extent do you use self-directed learning, informal learning and collaborative learning methods?
6. Where you use blended learning, did you create the blend on the basis of using multiple delivery media or multiple pedagogies? Are you clear about how the pedagogies you are using interact?

7. What is the current level of motivation and proactive engagement of your employees in self-directed learning activities?
8. What are likely to be the main pressures on these motivation and pro-activity levels in the future?
9. What has been the short-term impact of learning technologies on your learners' motivation? How has this changed over time?
10. What methods of scaffolding do you currently use? To what extent do you use scaffolding to target both learner-related issues (e.g. motivation, time management skills) and environment-related issues (e.g. time available for self-directed learning, managerial support)?

CONCLUDING THOUGHTS

We are on the brink of a breakthrough – a reconceptualisation of what corporate learning can achieve and do for organisations. The caveat, however, is that in order to step forward into this brave new world and deliver on all the promise, corporate learning functions are going to have to start approaching learning differently. Faced with the twin challenges of having to navigate a proliferation of new technologies and the raised expectations that will inevitably accompany them, learning functions will need the stabilising influence and piercingly pragmatic focus that a consideration of pedagogy brings. It is the map by which we can and surely must find our way. And it is something that we, as corporate learning professionals, must bring to the equation because if we don't, no one else will. Learning providers are likely to continue to bring a focus on technology. Business leaders will continue to bring a focus on their commercial needs. It is past time for corporate learning functions to start bringing balance through a focus on learning pedagogy.

This pedagogical focus will also be important for fending off the inevitable, and potentially damaging, backlash that is likely to accompany these new technologies. To some extent, we are already seeing this backlash. Some scholars argue that students do not achieve 'higher level' learning in online courses, and others suggest that technology use can in itself be harmful. For example, there have been research reports suggesting that the way we use computers is limiting our ability to apply ourselves properly to a single task and that frequent use of Internet search engines may negatively impact memory ability. Yet whatever the merits of these arguments, there is no going back on technological advances and no way to avoid them. And there is also research showing strong counter-findings – that even mild use of certain types of computer games can improve elements of intellectual functioning, such as the ability to multi-task and visual-spatial attention. Further research is required on all sides, of course, and the role of corporate learning in such developments must be to provide a steadying influence, not by simply avoiding innovation as appears to be common now, but by approaching new technologies through the lens of how they can or cannot be used to deliver learning.

In the previous chapter, I emphasised the need to be less led by the traditions of academic learning and instead become more focused on behaviour change and the commercial realities of performance improvement. In this chapter, I have highlighted how corporate learning functions will need to become more focused on pedagogy in order to deliver on these things, and how learning can change behaviour and improve performance. In the next chapter I look at the implications of all this on how corporate learning functions are resourced.

5 Resourcing learning solutions: people, people, people

The capability – or lack thereof – of HR staff has been much talked about in recent years. The discussion has largely focused on whether traditional HR professionals have the right skills and experiences to meet the challenges now facing the modern HR function. The leading HR bodies – the Chartered Institute of Personnel and Development (CIPD) in the UK and the Society for Human Resource Management (SHRM) in the United States – plus key HR commentators, such as Dave Ulrich, have challenged HR to develop new competencies and redefine its roles to focus on results and the value it can add to organisations.

At the heart of this debate, and pushing it forward all the time, is the notion that what counts as 'HR work' is gradually but persistently evolving. Changes such as the devolution of responsibility for elements of HR work to line managers, the centralisation of administrative HR activities into HR shared services, and the adoption of 'e-HR' integrated systems have brought with them new challenges and also new resourcing requirements. Indeed, HR resourcing is changing indelibly, with an influx of people without traditional HR backgrounds and the rapid growth of HR outsourcing. Simply put, HR isn't what it used to be.

Much the same can be said of the learning profession, too. There is certainly no shortage of change in the field. But compared with all that has been written about the what, how and who of HR resourcing, there is relatively little on how to resource corporate learning functions. This is surprising because although not all learning functions report to HR, the skills required have historically been associated with HR. And it is interesting because, as already noted, corporate learning and the people operating in this

97

space are under the spotlight as never before, and at a time when learning roles are becoming more difficult and complex. The recent downturn, coupled with the introduction of new technologies and informal learning pedagogies, has driven a move towards leaner functions, reducing staff-to-learner ratios from 6.7 learning professionals for every 1,000 learners in 2006 to just 5.2 in 2012.[76] This ratio reduction means that roles are now broader and there is greater pressure on individual capability, but there is also greater demand for technical skills. Broader plus more technical is a tough combination, and it is making deciding what types and combinations of people you need, not to mention actually finding them, increasingly challenging.

Chapters 3 and 4 focused on the what and the how of learning. This chapter is about the who. It is critical because recent research has shown that more than half of the variation in the impact of corporate learning functions on businesses is driven by differences in individual learning staff capabilities.[77] So we will look at what kinds of people and skills you need, the implications of this for the typical roles required in the modern corporate learning function, and whether, what and how to outsource. Let's begin by taking a step back and focusing on how the challenges facing modern corporate learning functions are changing and the consequences this has for resourcing them.

THE CHANGING CHALLENGE OF CORPORATE LEARNING DELIVERY

Defining what corporate learning functions do is not as easy as it used to be. For starters, the scope of corporate learning is expanding and integrating with talent management, change management and knowledge management,[78] sometimes to subsume these fields and at others to be subsumed by them. The recession has also wrought changes, heightening the pressure on learning organisations to be more cost-effective, more technologically savvy and more aligned with the needs of the business.

Looking at the HR population more broadly, the general consensus among commentators is that to successfully adapt to the changes facing the function, HR will need to become more strategic, more analytical (in terms of providing data-based insights) and more focused on results and value creation. And by and large this view holds for learning professionals as well. Yet I believe that the challenge for corporate learning professionals runs deeper because there are changes afoot in the fundamental tasks of corporate learning functions – in what learning means and entails in a corporate context – that will have significant repercussions for resourcing them. Three task changes, in particular, stand out.

From knowledge acquisition to performance-enhancing change

First and foremost, the purpose of corporate learning today is no longer learning, but change. For learning to be successful, something has to change as a result of the learning, and not just anything, but something that positively impacts performance. Today's corporate learning functions are achieving this in three ways. First, and as already noted, learning outcomes are increasingly being perceived less in terms of the acquisition of knowledge or skills and more in terms of concrete, sustained and performance-enhancing behaviour change. Second, the shift in focus from individual learning goals to organisational learning objectives has driven learning functions increasingly to become a critical lever in culture change initiatives. Companies such as BP and Barclays are good examples of this. They have developed learning solutions designed to increase the focus on performance in management conversations and shift the business culture in terms of how able people feel to challenge poor performance. At one level these initiatives may be about behaviour, but to have sustained impact they need to deliver massive shifts in corporate culture. Finally, as learning functions have moved into the field of knowledge management and the facilitation of informal learning processes, they are increasingly becoming synonymous with enabling innovation and continuous improvement: with doing things differently. Together, these three factors mean that, more than ever before, learning is not about acquiring knowledge, but about change – about enabling it, driving it and managing it. And for a function with a tendency to be process-driven with a historical focus on knowledge and skills, this shift is significant and challenging.

From aligning with businesses to helping businesses make money

Turn the clock back ten or fifteen years and the talk was of how learning professionals needed to get to know their businesses better in order to ensure that learning offerings were closely aligned with business performance drivers. That advice still holds. But I would go further. When I say learning functions are becoming more business-focused, I mean that the business of learning is becoming more like, well, a business. This runs counter to corporate learning's roots in education and its traditional philosophy of personal development, and indeed to many ears it may sound alien or heretical to talk of learning as a business. But with over $200 billion spent on corporate learning per year globally, like it or not, it *is* a business, and organisations are increasingly expecting their learning functions to act like one.

Most corporate learning functions are unlikely to follow in the path of IBM and turn their own internal learning initiatives into products that they sell externally, but it does happen and can be seen as the culmination of the call for HR and learning functions to focus on how they can provide value for their organisations. Research is thus showing how learning executives are increasingly being measured in terms of how well they manage the business side of learning, such as their ability to prove business impact, manage budgets and increase access to learning while reducing costs.[79] This trend can also be seen in my suggestion in Chapter 3 that learning needs analyses should be replaced by learning proposals that use cost–benefit analyses to place a value on learning (preferably a monetary one) and provide insights into how to improve business performance. The core tasks of learning may not have changed much – after all, it still needs designing, organising and delivering – but the approach corporate learning functions need to take and the skills they need to have are fundamentally changing.

From being technology-led to leveraging technology

In the previous two chapters I have argued that learning should not be led by technology trends. Instead it should be driven by what behaviour needs to change and how that change can best be produced – by outcomes and pedagogies rather than the alluring shine of new technologies. But there is a caveat: the world is changing, technology is becoming a core part of it, and learning functions need to be able to leverage this technology. Indeed, the fundamental task of learning functions has evolved to include producing or providing learning technologies that businesses can use, rather than merely using technologies to enable learning. Many corporate learning functions simply outsource this task, some work in partnership with their organisation's technology function, and others employ their own technology teams. Whatever your approach, if you work in learning, technology is part of what you need to manage, leverage and do.

MEETING THE RESOURCE CHALLENGE

Together, these shifts in the fundamental tasks of corporate learning functions are producing new challenges for their staff. Unfortunately, these challenges are also revealing some key deficiencies in how well equipped we are as a professional body to deal with them. As I noted in Chapter 1, only 17 per cent of surveyed business leaders report that they are 'very satisfied' with the performance of their learning functions,[80] and more than half of line managers believe that employee performance would not change if the learning function were eliminated today.[81] It is tempting to shrug off the perceived lack of quality as bias or stereotyping, but there is also more solid and worrying evidence that is not easily dismissed. For instance, the database of a leading assessment provider – YSC – shows that it has found that learning professionals on average have more 'experience' (for their level) than people from other functions or business areas, but they have significantly less 'overall capability' and less 'potential'. The lack of potential is particularly worrying as it suggests that things aren't about to improve anytime soon.

There therefore seems to be some basis to the prevailing perception that, as functions, HR more generally and learning specifically tend to have less capable people than other areas of the business. Depressingly, this is a perception held as much inside these functions as by external observers. For example, one of the UK's leading HR figures has recently publicly warned that the quality of HR senior leadership is declining and that the profession is losing influence. This appears to be even more of an issue for learning functions, where there are anecdotal reports of individuals being sent to lead learning functions not because of their sterling track record, but because learning is seen as a kind of career graveyard, an 'easy' HR role where the impact of their limited ability will be minimised.

Even if we put the overall quality issue to one side, the question remains of whether today's cadre of learning professionals has the right skill mix. For example, a recent survey showed that 42 per cent of HR and learning professionals reported that they were perceived as having a low level of business acumen by their colleagues, another revealed a lack of numerical and data-analytical skills, and repeated case studies have shown that learning staff generally lack the right project management, technical and systems implementation skills required to successfully manage large and complex IT projects.

Generally speaking, therefore, corporate learning functions are perceived as lacking in talent and essential skills. Inevitably, organisations are looking elsewhere to fill the gaps. Outsourcing is one solution, with access to skills being the most frequently cited benefit. And the sourcing of non-HR professionals is another solution. Sometimes this is seen as a way of ensuring the required levels of key technical skills, as is the case with some high profile appointments of former academics, such as Steve Kerr at GE and Goldman

Sachs, who prior to these roles was dean of the faculty of the USC business school; and the nomination of Joel Podolney, previously dean of Yale University business school, to head up Apple University. Other times, this is done to ensure the alignment of learning with business need, as is the case with the increasingly reported phenomenon of assigning commercial business leaders to corporate learning functions.

Yet these gap-filling moves, although sometimes successful, are too often impromptu improvisations rather than strategic moves: short-term reactions to what are ultimately long-term challenges. Often a broad overview of the key skills required in the modern corporate learning function is lacking, along with an appreciation of how these skills map onto core roles, and an understanding of what the impact and longer-term consequences of the various resourcing models can be. Let's now look at these issues, beginning with the kinds of people and skills you need.

KEY SKILLS REQUIRED

When thinking about people and skills, you need to consider not only the usual competency aspects – such as intelligence, drive and interpersonal skills – but also some learning-specific competencies. In fact, I suggest there are ten. Depending upon the scope of learning services in your organisation you may not require them all, but the following list is intended to help you think about which skills are essential in your context. It is not intended to be a complete list or a detailed competency framework; rather it is an indicative summary of key areas of expertise required.

Business acumen

Probably the single most talked about competency for HR and learning professionals these days is business acumen. Unfortunately, the volume of conversation has not translated into actual capability: recent CIPD research reports that three-fifths of HR professionals believe that HR functions still need to develop a better understanding

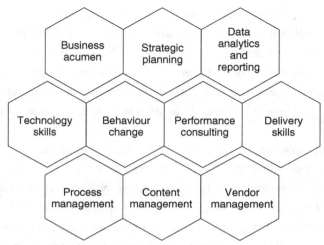

FIGURE 5.1 Ten key learning competencies

of business issues.[82] Without business acumen, individuals are fundamentally limited in their ability to develop insights and solutions that will work and prove valuable to the business.

Definitions of business acumen are a dime a dozen, but generally consist of two elements: the ability to understand things such as financials and value chains, and the ability to see how to create value. Where acumen does exist, understanding financials is a far more common attribute than understanding how to create value, and – insofar as it is related to entrepreneurship – there are some indications that the latter may be less easy to teach. I believe that all learning employees should understand financials to some extent, and almost all learning teams need at least one member who has some value creation skills. Fifteen years ago, business acumen was a side-note: today, it is a basic requisite. Indeed, research has noted the importance of having strong business acumen as a foundation for sound strategic planning.[83]

Strategic planning

Some of the most headline-hitting work on HR competencies – including those of learning professionals – in recent years has been

produced by Dave Ulrich. His key point is that what HR professionals do best and a lot of (maintaining good relationships with the business) has only a moderate impact on firm performance, whereas what
they do only moderately well and not often enough (namely strategic
contribution) has the potential to have a far greater impact.[84]

As a competency, strategic planning is generally considered to
have a number of components, including the ability to rise up from
the detail and take an overview, the capacity to take a long-term
view, and the capability to create clarity and distil a clear objective.
Having a plan ensures that there is direction and purpose to corporate learning activities, and makes sure that they support and enhance
the implementation of the broader business strategy. Without such a
plan, corporate learning activities are inevitably just a collection of
activities. Unsurprisingly, research has found higher levels of strategic planning ability in corporate learning functions that are perceived by their businesses to be higher performing. Obviously not all
your employees need to be able to develop a strategic plan, but your
function does need to have such a plan and your people need to be
able to understand it.

Data analytics and reporting

Another phrase that has been making headlines recently is 'insight-
driven HR'. Fuelled perhaps by a degree of marketing envy – awareness of the success of marketing functions in securing a role at many
top tables – some HR functions are trying to establish themselves
as the source of valuable people-related insights. To achieve this,
they are having to develop and source new or better skills in understanding, producing and using people metrics. This is more than
simple mathematical ability or familiarity with the latest statistics
software; it is about being able to use data to produce insights of
real value to the broader business. For corporate learning functions
there is an additional reason to have these skills, since the increased
focus on measurement and demonstrating value means they need to
develop their data analysis and reporting capabilities.[85] By tracking

data they can expose issues with cost structures and utilisation levels, as well as being able to assess the value and impact of learning on the business. Indeed, for many commentators, developing data reporting skills is a fundamental prerequisite for corporate learning functions to establish business credibility: all corporate learning staff should be comfortable with using data and there should be at least one data reporting expert in every team.

Performance consulting

Surveys report that more and more corporate learning functions are investing in building their employees' consulting skills to help them function effectively as business partners,[86] and recent years have witnessed an influx into corporate learning roles of individuals with consulting firm backgrounds. This focus on consulting skills is clearly critical if you have learning staff in business partner roles, but I am concerned about the current way consulting skills tend to be viewed, in particular the emphasis given to personal credibility.[87] Although I appreciate that credibility with internal customers is a real challenge for many learning professionals,[88] it is of limited value to individuals unless they use it to achieve something. To be truly effective learning professionals need to consult credibly and with purpose – with the end goal of performance in mind. Thus I refer to the fourth key competency not just as 'consulting' but as *performance consulting*: the ability to consult, work and negotiate with the business to improve the performance of individuals and businesses.

Behaviour change

As I have argued throughout this book, corporate learning in the twenty-first century needs to stop being about learning and to start being about behaviour change. As such, having people with a deep understanding of how to change behaviour is essential. In practice, this means an understanding of the learning pedagogies described in Chapter 4, an up-to-date awareness of corporate learning research, and knowledge of behaviour change techniques and methodologies from the fields of psychology, behavioural economics and psychotherapy. Moreover, I include in this competency the skills of *change champions*, who have the ability to initiate and sustain change at group and cultural levels as well as with individuals. It is not necessary for all your people to be behaviour change experts, but all should be familiar to some degree with the basic concepts and tenets. As a starting point, to gain a sense of how much people currently know, I recommend asking two fundamental questions: 'How do you change behaviour?' and 'How do you keep it changed?' In my experience, many learning professionals struggle to deliver a clear and sophisticated response to these questions. This needs to change.

Delivery

The single most changed facet of corporate learning is arguably delivery. Most traditional classroom instructors now find themselves spending much time outside a physical classroom – delivering training online and working with learners on a one-to-one basis.[89] Indeed, when we talk about delivery these days we are actually referring to four very different skills: instructional training delivery, group facilitation skills, coaching skills (both one-on-one and group) and collaboration support – the facilitation of online collaborative learning networks. Group facilitation skills are becoming increasingly important as learning functions move into more consultative roles. Likewise, the coaching of individual leaders by internal staff is on the rise. And although collaboration support may not sound like a skill in its own right, research shows that prior experience of supporting online collaboration is important for successfully intervening to stimulate online collaborative learning and avoid dysfunctional collaborative activities.[90] Obviously these skills are not equally important to all corporate learning functions, but even when a function outsources all delivery, some experience in this area is important in order to understand and manage the activity of external vendors. We may have come a long way, but the need for good old-fashioned classroom delivery skills has not gone away, nor will it.

Process management

Administrative skills have long been a key required skill in operationally focused learning functions, but the advent of Learning
Management Systems has changed these roles significantly – broad-
ening them, reducing the administrative burden, and adding an
element of project management. I call the result process management: the basic capacity to organise things and keep processes and
projects running smoothly, and for many corporate learning functions it remains a key required skill.

Content management

A related, but separate competency is content management or curation: the sourcing, management and governance of digitised information to maximise accessibility and ensure that only the best,
most useful information rises to the top. With the arrival of LMSs,
the increasing tendency to break learning into bite-sized chunks or
'learning objects', and the movement of learning functions into the
area of knowledge management, managing content is fast becoming a required skill. For evidence of its value, look no further than
Google.

   The challenge for corporate learning functions as they move
into this space is that there are two levels on which they can manage content. First, they can simply categorise it. Second, they can sift
it and organise it in terms of its potential value. For example, some
online services will sort through new articles from various business
journals and send you select pieces on a regular basis. On the face
of it, this sounds useful. However, some of the companies providing
this service merely categorise new articles, ask you which subjects
you're interested in and send you a few articles from the related category. This may have some utility, but it does nothing to ensure
the quality and potential value of the information reaching learners.
There are few simple solutions here, but the challenge is likely to be
a growing one for many corporate learning functions, and how well

they negotiate them is likely to be a key determinant of their level of success.

Vendor management

As we will discover later in the chapter, outsourcing has been a growing trend in corporate learning for many years as a solution to the issue of how to provide the required skills in a cost-effective way. As ever, with new solutions come new challenges, specifically in this case the need for corporate learning functions to have strong vendor management skills. Research has shown that having these skills is not only critical to achieving value through outsourcing but is also the single most significant factor within the purchaser's control.[91] Unfortunately, other research also shows that nearly half of HR professionals do not consider their vendor management skills to be any better than fair.[92] Although some people dislike the use of the word 'vendor', preferring alternatives like 'partnership', and although it is obviously necessary to have a partnership-like relationship with providers, I believe it is important to keep in mind the commercial nature of the relationship.

Technology skills

The final competency is a big one. As I have already noted, technology is a reality of the present and future of corporate learning. To successfully negotiate the opportunities and challenges it brings, corporate learning functions need to be aware of a number of elements. First, they need *technology proponents* – people who have the ability to use technologies new and old to deliver effective and efficient learning solutions. For all corporate learning functions this is and will remain fundamental. Not all people will be equally gifted in technology matters, but all need some degree of knowledge. Second, they require systems implementation know-how and expertise in managing complex IT projects. This is the most common capability gap facing corporate learning functions seeking to implement new technology-based learning solutions. Finally, for those corporate learning functions directly employing their own technology people and developing their own systems, IT and systems skills are also essential.

COMPETENCY IMPLICATIONS FOR KEY ROLES

Competency models such as the one in Figure 5.1 are useful as frameworks for considering skill requirements, assessing capability and structuring development, as well as providing focal points for establishing a benchmark of what strong capability looks like. But the driving force in resourcing is roles – the jobs that need doing. The key question the learning leader has to ask here is 'What business am I in?' If you are responsible for delivering hundreds of technical training programmes, the skills and roles your function requires will be similar to that of a manufacturing business. If your main focus is on organisational development and facilitating change, your function will more closely resemble a consultancy. And if your core competence is leadership development interventions, your function will be similar to a business school.

Since roles and the structures they form are so context dependent, it is not possible to provide a definitive list of what roles you should have. We can, however, look at some of the common key roles and explore the implications for such positions of the task changes and the required competencies described above. We will begin by looking at probably the most significant role – that of the chief learning officer.

The chief learning officer

When CEO Jack Welch gave Steve Kerr the title of chief learning officer in the mid 1990s, General Electric became the first company on record to have a learning executive with the CLO title. As CLO roles have proliferated they have inevitably begun to vary. At one end of the spectrum we find what are effectively training directors, while at the other end we find fully fledged strategic partners. Yet within this variation, commonality does exist.

In 2000, a study was published that explored the roles, priorities and performance measures of ten of the first wave of CLOs, and it concluded that their roles were largely strategic, focused on linking learning priorities and initiatives to the strategic direction of the firm.[93] For the most part, not a lot has changed since then.[94] Recent research conducted by the American Society for Training & Development found that the two tasks that CLOs devote the most time to, on average, are strategy development and communication with business executives, while the two criteria most heavily weighted in their performance evaluations are alignment with business strategy and contribution to business value (followed some way after by the efficiency of the learning function and budget management).[95] In meeting these objectives, the two biggest challenges CLOs report are measuring and communicating value and developing effective solutions to resource constraints. So the core objectives and challenges of most CLO roles seem to be clear, common and consistent.

There also appears to be some consensus on the skills required to meet the challenges of these roles. The competencies most frequently cited as critical are business acumen and strategic planning, and the ability to market and communicate the benefits of the learning function. However, it seems that learning executives are required to have an increasingly broad set of competencies in order to succeed.[96] Some recent research, for example, has looked at the impact of the changing scope of the corporate learning function on the role of the CLO and found that it is increasingly demanding expertise in:

- Business management – running the corporate learning function as a business.
- Performance management – focusing on employee performance and connecting it with business performance.
- Demographic management – ensuring the corporate learning strategy addresses current and future business challenges resulting from demographic shifts and supports different audiences' learning needs.
- Global leadership – managing the challenges created by the globalisation of learning.

This is a broad and tough set of competencies by any standards, although there is one glaring omission, namely thought leadership, which also hardly features in the literature. This raises a concern. CLOs have to spend an extraordinary amount of time on stakeholder management, and as a result, tend to end up a significant distance from the frontline of learning delivery. The only way they can function effectively in this environment is if they have an expert understanding of the challenges of behaviour change and the implementation of change programmes. So I am surprised to see so little mention of this basic requirement. Although I acknowledge that the emphasis on business understanding emerged because some learning leaders were disconnected from and not respected by their businesses, there is a very real danger that this emphasis will result in a generation of learning leaders who know how to talk a good talk, but do not understand the business of learning, are not educated consumers of the services provided by vendors, and lack the expertise to develop effective curricula. So using the competency list above, the four key competencies I see as essential for success in most CLO roles, based on my own experience in such roles and all that I have observed in the more or less successful careers of my peers, are: business acumen, strategic planning, performance consulting and behaviour change.

The career path of the CLO

We recently conducted an international study at IMD looking at the profiles and career paths of 182 learning leaders from around the world. They had an average age of 48, with 65 per cent being male and 35 per cent female. As a group they were highly educated and came from a wide range of educational backgrounds, the most common fields of study being business administration/management, psychology, natural sciences, engineering and social sciences. In terms of career background, the vast majority came from HR and learning roles. Interestingly, 44 per cent were external hires, new into the company, suggesting a general lack of depth or confidence in internal talent pools.

Even more interesting than where they came from is the question of the options open to them going forward. The vast majority stated they would want to move to another functional job in learning or HR. However, there are so few strategic jobs in learning (or indeed HR) that most of them will probably move to another company or into a career as an independent consultant, which appears to be the final destination for many. Thus there is a real danger that the very best of our profession's expertise will continually be lost to us, or at least siphoned off to consultancies.

Moreover, when we couple these issues with the anecdotal evidence that restructuring appears more common in learning functions than in technical disciplines (e.g. finance), we have a pretty disturbing picture in which it is difficult to attract the best people into the profession and even harder to keep them in it. The learning profession thus risks becoming a kind of professional ghetto that quality leaders briefly illuminate before disappearing into consultancy. The issue appears to be less who are today's executives and more who will be tomorrow's.

Implications for other roles

The pattern and definition of roles in corporate learning functions obviously differ, but looking across the board four main types of roles have historically existed.

- Learning manager – an internal consulting role similar to that of the HR business partner, usually aligned with particular business units or segments of the population, and focusing on identifying learning needs, implementing learning solutions and managing the relationship with the target population.
- Learning deliverer – traditionally focused on classroom delivery.
- Learning designer – sometimes referred to as instructional designer, dedicated to the development of learning solutions.
- Learning administrator – an administrative and project management role, sometimes with an element of customer service.

Today these roles are increasingly integrated and less commonly found as separate roles in their own right. For example, it has become relatively rare to find employees purely focused on learning delivery, and for the most part this work is either subsumed into other roles or outsourced. Before we look at what new roles may need to exist to meet the changing nature of corporate learning, let's take each of the historical roles in turn and look at how they have changed.

Learning manager

The key tasks of the learning manager role have tended to be managing the relationship with particular business segments and overseeing the implementation of key learning programmes. The role is therefore increasingly being described as business partnering or performance consultancy. Moreover, with the outsourcing of learning design and delivery in many organisations, the role has become broader than ever, incorporating oversight of these tasks and so requiring a greater knowledge of design principles, experience of delivery and expertise in partnering with external suppliers. As such, the key skills typically required for this role are performance consulting, behaviour change, business acumen and vendor management.

Learning designer

The traditional learning designer role seems to be going in one of two directions. In many organisations, the role is simply disappearing as the task of instructional design is outsourced, often with oversight and input from learning managers. In other organisations, though, the learning design role is being expanded to include curating content and elements of delivery such as managing online communities of practice and supporting the use of social media for learning. In such cases, it is therefore taking on quite a different profile, requiring expertise in four key skills: behaviour change, technology skills, content management and delivery skills.

Learning deliverer

As I have already noted, learning delivery is increasingly rare as a separate role in its own right, but traditional classroom training still takes place in most organisations and so the role continues to exist, especially in relation to skills or product training. It has, however, transformed in its breadth, not only in the range of delivery methods and media used but also in the increasing expectation of learners that their learning deliverer understands the realities of day-to-day business and has a degree of business acumen. To meet this breadth, the four key skills thus required of the modern learning deliverer are delivery skills, technology skills, behaviour change and business acumen.

Moreover, the learning delivery role increasingly includes internal resources who are not part of the learning function and do not have a traditional learning background. Examples include 'subject matter experts', mobilised from technical functions to develop networks of trained internal facilitators for programme delivery, and business leaders – from the CEO down – who are often called on to participate in key programmes. The most common aims here are to embed programmes within the business and ensure the credibility and relevance of the learning for learners. This approach can be highly useful, but it does need to be coupled with a proper programme of training and support for the selected leaders to equip them with the delivery skills and understanding of behaviour change that they need. In this regard, both IBM and Capgemini offer accreditation processes (see the case study at the end of this chapter).

Learning administrator
This role, although it still exists in its traditional form, is increasingly focused on managing LMS content and operation; ensuring a positive customer experience for LMS users; and – in some cases – project managing programme implementation. In some organisations, an element of content management also falls within this remit, as do aspects of vendor management – for example when learning administrators use the LMS to oversee the booking of participants into learning events delivered by external vendors. Finally, elements of event management are also being incorporated into the role – covering the orchestration of large, complex events that bring together

hundreds of people. The four key skills typically required for these roles are thus process management, technology skills, content management and vendor management.

New and additional roles

To deal with new challenges – many of them driven by technology – new and additional roles are appearing within corporate learning functions. Five in particular stand out:

- *Technology manager*: a role focused on maintaining internal learning technology systems and/or overseeing the management of external vendors providing such systems.
- *Content manager*: with the 'chunk-ification' of learning into 'learning objects' and corporate learning functions' move into knowledge management, an increasing number of organisations are employing a specialised content manager or knowledge curator.
- *Data manager*: lacking specialised skills in data analytics elsewhere in their team, but in desperate need of them, some learning functions are now employing data gurus to help them track, analyse and report learning metrics.
- *Portfolio manager*: in larger organisations or where learning programmes have been split into many smaller pieces, a person may be employed to oversee the whole portfolio of offerings, rationalizing them and periodically eliminating duplication or retiring programmes that are no longer needed.
- *Communities manager*: in organisations that use online communities and social media in their learning programmes, new 'communities' roles are being created to provide the specialised skills to oversee and facilitate these media. These roles are usually filled either by individuals from traditional learning delivery backgrounds or by technical subject matter experts, who stimulate and facilitate online discussion and work to ensure it stays on track and produces valuable outputs.

Defining corporate learning function roles

Key questions you need to know the answers to in order to be assured that you have the skills you need

---

1. Who will manage the relationship with the business or segments of it, and do they have sufficient expertise in performance consulting, business acumen and behaviour change?
2. Do you have sufficient project management experience available to ensure the smooth development, implementation and management of learning initiatives? Will this fall to learning administrators, learning managers or both?
3. Do you have the skills you will need to track, analyse and report key learning metrics?
4. Do your internal and external learning deliverers have expertise and experience in the types of delivery that you will need? For example, do you need specialist skills in managing online communities and informal learning processes?
5. Will your internal and external learning deliverers have credibility with learners in terms of understanding the business?
6. Who will oversee evaluations, so that you can demonstrate the value of learning initiatives? Is it part of the responsibility of your learning managers or of those who are in charge of the delivery of your programmes?
7. Who will manage relationships with vendors and do they have the appropriate skills to act on behalf of your organisation?

It is clear that as a result of changes in the fundamental tasks facing corporate learning functions and the consequent changes in the required skills, traditional learning roles are changing – and not in a way that makes resourcing any easier. Generally, they are all becoming broader, more pressured and more complex. It is little surprise that 50 per cent of organisations report finding it difficult to recruit good learning professionals with the skills they require. The new breed of learning managers appears especially difficult to recruit, since they need business understanding in combination with both consulting and technical behaviour change skills.

KEY RESOURCING CONSIDERATIONS

Having looked at how the changing nature of corporate learning is transforming the skills corporate learning functions require and the roles they need to perform, let us now look at four of the key issues organisations face in filling these roles.

Buy or grow

The decision on the perennial issue of whether to buy or grow is typically driven by availability: the skill set of current staff, the perceived developability of key skills, and the urgency of the need. So which skills can be developed in almost everyone and quickly? Research on this is lacking, but Table 5.1 serves as a quick reference guide.

Seeking to upgrade their learning capability, and being unclear how to develop their existing staff or simply not having the time required to do so, many organisations are buying the skills they need – bringing new people into the function. Probably the clearest example of this is the recent trend of bringing commercial people into learning functions in order to increase levels of business acumen. Although this approach can be useful, if corporate learning functions are to avoid continued reliance on the external market for sourcing skills, they need to ensure that any policy of buying is balanced by one of growing. This is also important for tackling the issue of dwindling career options for learning professionals, in the face of the need for new skills and the intrusion of non-learning professionals into their career space.

Such programmes are much needed, too, as learning professionals have often fallen prey to 'cobbler's children syndrome'. Like the children of shoemakers, who often go without shoes, learning professionals focus on helping others to learn but neglect their own needs in this respect. The situation could be exacerbated in future, as the learning profession increasingly seems to straddle disciplines and so often falls between them: certainly when looking at learning providers, there are very few targeted offerings for learning professionals. The HR bodies in the United States and UK – the SHRM and CIPD, respectively – have such offerings, of course, but their

Table 5.1 *Developing competencies*

Specific skill		How easy to develop? (i.e. can everyone do it?)	How quick to develop?
Business acumen	Understanding	Easier	Quicker
	Value creation	Harder	Slower
Strategic planning	Take a broad overview	Harder	Slower
	Take a long-term view	Harder	Slower
	Distil objectives	Harder	Slower
Data analytics and reporting	Numerical analytical ability	Harder	Quicker
	Producing data-based insights	Harder	Slower
	Evaluation	Easier	Quicker
Performance consulting	Relationship management	Harder	Quicker
	Performance improvement	Easier	Slower
	Negotiation and influencing	Easier	Quicker
Behaviour change	Individual level	Easier	Slow
	Group level	Easier	Slow
	Cultural level	Easier	Slow
Delivery skills	Instructional training	Easier	Quicker
	Group facilitation	Easier	Slower
	Coaching	Easier	Slower
	Collaboration support	Easier	Quicker
Process management	Administration	Easier	Quicker
	Project management	Harder	Quicker

Table 5.1 (*cont.*)

Specific skill		How easy to develop? (i.e. can everyone do it?)	How quick to develop?
Content management	Content organisation	Harder	Quicker
	Facilitation of social content development	Easier	Quicker
Vendor management	Vendor management	Easier	Quicker
Technology skills	Technology use	Easier	Quicker
	Technology implementation	Easier	Slower
	System design	Harder	Slower

primary focus is the main body of HR professionals rather than learning specialists. Specialist organisations do exist, such as the American Society for Training & Development, and numerous networks for sharing learning have emerged, such as those associated with CLO Magazine, LinkedIn and the roundtable networks of the top business schools such as IMD. Yet overall, the offerings have been exceptionally sparse and not particularly high quality, as evidenced by the buzz surrounding two new entrants into the field: the University of Pennsylvania's Master's and Doctoral programmes for CLOs; and the CLIP accreditation process offered by the European Foundation for Management Development, which seeks to accredit corporate learning functions through a rigorous assessment and peer-review process.

Although there are encouraging signs that the situation might improve, growing learning professionals is not as easy as might be expected. With this in mind, some organisations are balancing their buying in of new skills with the implementation of formal programmes to help support learning. Research has shown that most learning professionals learn the methods, technologies and techniques of learning on the job, from peers or from existing solutions in place within their organisations. Programmes are therefore being established that promote such on-the-job learning, for example through the use of organised 'scrum teams' that bring together learning staff with different skillsets to work on particular projects and thereby give exposure to new challenges and opportunities to learn. However, although learning on the job is excellent for developing practical expertise and experience, such programmes do need to be balanced with support for staff in keeping their expertise up to date. The last decade has seen an exponential rise in research into learning and development, and staying abreast of all the new findings and theories can be extremely difficult amid the pressures of day-to-day activity, especially in a field as diverse as learning.

Relationship to HR

Related to the above issue and key to learning resourcing is the relationship to HR: namely, do you seek to source talent inside HR or outside of it? This is particularly pertinent for CLO and learning manager roles, where there is a strong element of interface with the business. Although I do not believe that *all* learning professionals should have a background in corporate learning or HR, I am also concerned that too often non-HR personnel – selected for their business acumen and experience in implementing large programmes – are being appointed to senior learning roles, but without sufficient planning, support and follow-through to ensure that they develop the requisite technical functional skills. To perform effectively in these roles, individuals need to be credible to their business audience, but they also need to have technical functional skills in order to do something with their credibility.

Part of the issue here is the spate of research showing that business acumen has significantly more impact on learning staff performance than technical learning expertise.[97] These studies have hit the headlines and helped stoke an apparent obsession with learning professionals being 'business savvy' above all else. Yet if we go back to the original research on the matter, it was clear that although business knowledge should be viewed as a basic credential to operate in this space, it should not be seen as an alternative to technical ability. The enthusiasm for business acumen and the consequent lack of focus on technical ability is thus of special concern to me, since I believe that many if not most corporate learning functions need to redevelop their functional skills – to move away from traditional learning and toward learning as behaviour change and performance improvement. Knowing how to get things done is critical, but it is of limited value without also knowing what you're doing.

Geographical and cultural differences

A further consideration for many corporate learning functions is how to accommodate regional differences in capability levels and need. For example, in emerging markets such as South Africa, India and China, learning professionals tend to be recruited on the basis of their operational and business partnering skills, whereas in some more mature markets these skills are seen as basic table stakes on top of which further skills are then sought (such as business acumen). CLOs must therefore take regional differences into account in their resourcing decisions and, when planning functional development initiatives, make sure to lift everyone up to the same standards on the one hand, while respecting local demand on the other.

Internal versus external

When neither buying nor growing is feasible, organisations have one option left: to go external. This is one of the most significant strategic and structural decisions a CLO can make – whether to keep roles internal or to outsource them. By 'outsourcing', I mean both the procurement of end-to-end processes (outsourcing) and the procurement of specific, discrete projects or elements of tasks (out-tasking). It arises either when the use of an internal supplier is discontinued or when new services are purchased that were not previously pro-vided in-house. The size of the corporate learning outsourcing indus-try is not exactly known, but it is substantial and growing.[98] In fact, research shows that it is consistently placed in the top two HR ser-vices most commonly outsourced.[99] Post-downturn data suggests that over 90 per cent of learning function departments outsource at least some of their work[100] and that on average they spend around 25 per cent of their budgets on outsourcing.[101]

Unsurprisingly, plenty has been written about outsourcing, with a 2009 study finding over 22,000 articles on the subject.[102] That's a lot of reading. Yet very little of this has been independent research; the vast majority of what has been written is consultant reports or articles in the popular press. Indeed, only a handful of studies have systematically measured the impact of outsourcing. This means that in all likelihood most outsourcing decisions have been and are still being taken without independently verified understanding of when, where and how outsourcing can deliver value. Given the size of the outsourcing market, this is pretty horrifying.

THE LOWDOWN ON OUTSOURCING

Having looked at how the changing nature of corporate learning is transforming the skills corporate learning functions require, the roles they need to perform, and the key issues facing them in these roles, let us now look in more depth at outsourcing, one of the most popular solutions to these challenges. Specifically, what does the available independent research say about who is outsourcing, what they are outsourcing, the potential benefits, the risks involved and how best to go about it?

Who is outsourcing?

Private sector organisations are generally more likely both to outsource learning tasks and to use larger numbers of suppliers than their public sector counterparts.[103] Within the private sec-tor, smaller firms outsource more than larger organisations,[104] and organisations with decentralised training budgets show a greater likelihood to outsource learning tasks than organisations with centrally held budgets.[105] A 2005 study looking across the gamut of HR outsourcing identified three main groups of companies using outsourcing:[106]

- Smaller companies that do not find it necessary or possible to have internal learning professionals.
- Companies that have internal learning professionals, but outsource some learning tasks in order to save staff time.
- Companies that have internal learning professionals, but outsource the learning tasks for which they lack in-house expertise.

It should be noted that none of these factors has been demonstrated to be related to outsourcing outcomes: for instance, smaller firms may outsource more, but they appear no more or less satisfied with the result of outsourcing than larger companies.[107]

What are they outsourcing?

It is a fair bet that almost any and every aspect of learning that can be outsourced has been by someone. Only a small proportion of organisations outsource all of their training – somewhere between 2 per cent and 8 per cent of organisations, depending upon which survey you believe.[108] The four activities most commonly outsourced, in approximate order, are: learning content design and development, learning delivery, learning technology infrastructure, and learning evaluation.[109] In addition, there are reports that organisations are increasingly using external providers for content modification (i.e. converting content to e-learning) and content localisation (i.e. adapting content for use across multiple global locations).[110]

Why are they outsourcing? What are the potential benefits?

In an interesting analysis of the reasons organisations decide to outsource, both within and beyond HR, a 2002 study identified four broad kinds of benefits:[111]

- Financial – including cost savings and cost control.
- Business and strategic – such as process re-engineering, the ability to focus on core tasks, and enabling rapid standardisation across organisations.
- Technical – typically including increased expertise, improved services and new technologies.
- Political – such as reducing the influence and control of particular executives or decentralised business segments.

Much of the research into outsourcing benefits has of course been conducted by outsourcing providers. The most common benefits they advertise are lower costs, better service quality and access to expertise. Beyond this, other benefits described include:

- freeing up staff to focus on core, value-adding tasks;
- standardisation and consistency;
- enabling roll-out of learning initiatives in overseas locations;
- increased flexibility to accommodate changes in demand;
- the purchase of intellectual capital;
- increased innovation.

So that's the theory and the hype, but what are the facts? What are the real reasons organisations decide to outsource learning tasks, and what benefits do they realise? Well, the key reasons cited by organisations for their outsourcing decisions do indeed appear to be costs, expertise and quality. However, although cost-cutting has historically been seen as the key driver of outsourcing, it no longer appears to be the dominant factor in most organisations' decision-making. Instead, surveys consistently show that, generally, the key reason organisations outsource aspects of learning is to gain access to skills and knowledge. Given the competency challenges described above, this is not surprising. There do appear to be some geographical variations in this, of course. There are some suggestions that cost reduction could be a more influential factor in the United States, and there are specific locations and scenarios where it is *the* factor. For example, in Switzerland it is common for companies to outsource some or all of their apprenticeship training activities to external service providers in order to benefit from the economies of scale that these providers can achieve.[112]

And what of the benefits realised? Looking at the independent research, one thing seems clear: although outsourcing learning can yield benefits, the circumstances under which it is most beneficial or can offer specific benefits have not yet been determined. However, in one study that appears representative of the general findings, a majority of outsourcing purchasers reported an improvement in content design (62 per cent) and content delivery (51 per cent), although only 29 per cent experienced a reduction in costs.[113] Thus, although there are circumstances in which cost savings can be significant, a good rule of thumb seems to be that outsourcing has a bigger impact on quality than on costs. So if you are going to outsource, make sure it is for the right reasons.

Why should they not outsource? What are the potential risks?

Although the majority of outsourcing purchasers appear satisfied with the performance of their suppliers, only about one-third report being 'very satisfied', and there is some evidence that this proportion is decreasing – perhaps as a result of the increase in purchasers' expectations that tends to accompany market maturation. Yet there is more to it than just increasing expectations. For example, a 2004 study by the US-based SHRM reported that in 25 per cent of cases HR outsourcing led to a decrease in quality.[114] Estimates of outsourcing failure rates vary, but a significant body of research shows that many outsourcing relationships do not achieve the expected results.[115] Which begs the question of why.

The issues are manifold, but fall into two broad categories: those to do with either the supplier or the purchaser of outsourcing. The issues related to the outsourcing supplier begin with the risks of picking the wrong supplier. For example, since access to expertise is a key driver of outsourcing, many purchasers may not have an informed view on the expertise of potential suppliers. Even when a good vendor is picked, inexperience in purchasing outsourcing can lead to unbalanced contracts, which can create problems later on in the relationship. These issues typically revolve around intellectual copyright and exit clauses. For instance, it is common for outsourcing suppliers to seek to retain copyright of materials that they design exclusively for the purchaser at the purchaser's cost, which can limit the ability of the purchaser to switch providers later if it is not happy with the delivery of this content. Beyond the selection and contracting issues, the most commonly reported challenges are the inability of external suppliers to fully understand the internal corporate culture; a decline in consultant quality over time (as the best or most senior ones move on to new clients); and suppliers engaging in opportunistic behaviour. Examples of such behaviour include exaggerated price increases at contract renewal, charging excessively for adjustments or add-ons during the contract period, and cutting costs by reducing service quality in areas where outcomes are not thoroughly specified.

The second broad category of issues relates to the outsourcing purchaser. For example, the most frequently reported problem in the outsourcing relationship reported by suppliers is the inability of purchasers to express and describe in detail what they require.[116] A related issue is learning professionals' lack of vendor management skills. A third issue is a potential weakening of the relationship between the corporate learning function and the organisation, in particular a reduction in the understanding of learning needs, due to the supplier effectively taking over part of the relationship.

Finally, and a particularly worrying issue for many organisations, is that outsourcing specific activities inevitably limits the in-house development of competencies related to those activities. As a result, organisations can find themselves caught in a vicious cycle: they outsource to access expertise, but this removes the opportunity to hire or develop the expertise themselves, and they continue to rely on outsourcing to fill the skill gap. Indeed, I have witnessed some of the world's largest companies fall into this trap, to the extent that they have to use external third parties to monitor the outsourcing supplier's performance as they do not have the expertise to do so themselves. Thus, one of the biggest concerns organisations have about outsourcing learning is loss of control and finding themselves overly dependent upon suppliers, as many surveys have found.

So outsourcing learning, although it can yield benefits – most notably access to specialised expertise and an improvement in service quality – is also fraught with challenges. Organisations that rush in to outsourcing are therefore more likely to experience the potential downsides than to gain the potential benefits. Yet almost all of the challenges identified above can easily be managed or mitigated against. So let's now look at what the independent research shows works best when engaging and managing outsourcing suppliers.

What works best?

As I have described, outsourcing successfully is not easy and, since so much depends on context, there is no single recipe for success. However, drawing on the independent research and my own experiences, I have identified ten clear recommendations to consider when undertaking any outsourcing.

Be clear

Simply put, organisations that set clear objectives and targets are more likely to achieve them. Organisations that have more detailed contractual agreements with learning suppliers are more likely to report higher levels of supplier performance, more effective design and delivery of learning, and higher satisfaction levels. Moreover, the more clearly contracts lay out targets, performance indicators and penalties, the less chance there is of opportunistic behaviour subsequently occurring.

Avoid poor selection decisions

When selecting suppliers it seems that the characteristics deemed most important are typically the supplier's knowledge of the organisation and its industry, their ability to deliver and to deliver quickly, and – inevitably – cost.[117] In my experience, when companies make the wrong selection decision it is typically for one of three reasons. First, they overly rely on existing relationships – picking a supplier they know well without considering carefully enough the supplier's capability. Second, they select only on cost, to the exclusion of all other considerations. And finally, they ignore the element of trust – what their intuition says about whether they like and have confidence in the supplier (my rule of thumb is to assume that something will go wrong at some point and ask which supplier I would most like by my side when that happens).

Test your selection decisions
I never cease to be amazed by the number of organisations that speak very highly of their suppliers, but have no hard, internally produced data to back this up. All too often, purchasers either do not evaluate the quality of their suppliers' work sufficiently, or even leave this to the suppliers themselves. I consider evaluation and governance in more detail in Chapters 6 and 8, so suffice to say you should have a clear structure and plan for evaluation and governance and neither of them should ever be outsourced.

Leverage market forces in managing suppliers
It is common for organisations to use multiple suppliers, yet few have an active plan to leverage the market forces that can be created by having more than one supplier. This is a lost opportunity, since research has shown that the market forces created by enabling competition between suppliers can produce improved service levels and reduced costs.[118] There are three things in particular that organisations can do here. First, don't let the supplier pool grow too large. I have seen some companies with literally hundreds of suppliers. In this situation it can be almost impossible to compare suppliers, and if there's no comparison, there's no competition. Second, measure the performance of your suppliers. And third, make this performance data widely available and an integral part of your supplier selection decisions.

Beware closed systems

One way corporate learning functions often seek to control the quality of learning outsourcing across diverse business units is to use preferred supplier lists. Although these lists have their benefits, I also have concerns with them. First, if you use them, it is critical to have a mechanism for promoting new suppliers onto the list and relegating existing suppliers from it. Without such a mechanism your ability to apply market pressures to suppliers will be limited. Second, determined business units can almost always find ways around centrally set supplier lists, thereby undermining their utility. One solution here can be to focus on the how of outsourcing rather than the who, by setting mandated contracting processes and standardised terms and conditions rather than a defined list of suppliers. This approach allows business units the freedom to select who they want while ensuring consistent standards are set.

Onboard your suppliers

Having selected a supplier, it is critical to have an onboarding plan for them: a thorough briefing about the business and their key stakeholders within it. In my experience, many businesses tend to assume the supplier has business knowledge so they skip this step. Yet without an onboarding plan, it can be challenging to ensure that suppliers have the necessary level of understanding about the business and its culture to develop and deliver effective learning solutions.

Plan for change

This may sound obvious, but one of the key challenges outsourcing buyers face is managing subsequent change in the internal organisation. Post-outsourcing, roles and responsibilities change, reporting relationships can shift, and most of those involved will need to perform new tasks or the same tasks in different ways. Planning and support for such changes, although essential, is too often overlooked.

Invest in vendor management skills

Related to the above, vendor management seems to be the area in which those embarking on outsourcing struggle the most, yet research clearly shows that it is also the single most significant factor within the purchaser's control for ensuring successful outsourcing outcomes.[119] Assuming that learning employees have these skills or leaving this aspect to the procurement department is unfortunately the norm here. As a result, only a minority of learning professionals report feeling capable in this area. Investing in acquiring vendor management skills is thus vital.

Communication is key

Research has almost unequivocally established a firm link between effective communication and successful outsourcing relationships. Thus, organisations that report higher performance levels from their outsourcing suppliers and higher overall satisfaction levels with their outsourcing relationships also report having more frequent discussions with these suppliers.[120]

Have an exit strategy

There's an old proverb that asserts 'Prepare for the worst and hope for the best', and I think this is good advice when it comes to outsourcing. Before entering any outsourcing relationship, it is prudent to be clear on your exit strategy. Particularly pertinent issues here are effective contractual clauses to ensure a smooth exit and a plan to manage the impact of outsourcing on internal capability levels. Without a thorough strategy, issues such as these can effectively tie organisations into outsourcing relationships that are failing to deliver value and make the organisations perpetually dependent upon external suppliers. And dependency should always be a choice.

Outsourcing checklist

1. Before seeking a supplier, do you have clear and specific objectives for the work to be outsourced?
2. Are you inviting proposals from multiple suppliers, including some you have not done business with before?
3. Are your supplier selection criteria clear?
4. Do you have the expertise you need to evaluate the potential suppliers' capability?

5. Does your contract clearly stipulate targets, performance indicators and penalties?

6. Do you have a supplier evaluation plan in place and specified in the contract?

7. Where you have multiple suppliers operating in the same space, how will you create and leverage market pressures?

8. Do you have a supplier onboarding process in place?

9. Do you have a change plan in place to support your company's switch to the supplier?

10. Have you trained your staff in managing suppliers?

11. Do you have regular communication points established with your suppliers?

12. What is your exit strategy? What is the cost associated with an early exit from the contract?

CONCLUDING THOUGHTS

Obtaining the right person for the job is always important. If you don't get this right, it doesn't usually end well. And to have any hope of finding the right person, you first need to know what you need from them. In this chapter, I have looked at how changes in the challenges facing modern corporate learning functions are having a significant impact on the types of skills and roles that organisations need. We have seen how the pressures to focus on behaviour change, to treat corporate learning like a business, and to leverage technology are all changing the landscape of corporate learning careers. And we have seen how CLOs need to perform a number of careful balancing acts in addressing their resourcing needs: between commercial and technical skills, between buying and growing, and between insourcing and outsourcing. Yet we have also seen how many if not most of the challenges can be successfully met or mitigated with forethought and careful planning. Resourcing is a critical issue and not least because, with little in the way of effective learning evaluation being conducted at present, the selection of people and/or suppliers for a particular role or task is probably the single most important piece of quality assurance that organisations currently engage in. And it is to this issue that I will turn in the next chapter: how organisations can best evaluate the effectiveness of what they do and demonstrate its value to the business.

Case study: Capgemini University: facilitating high quality learning

Capgemini, the global consulting, technology and professional services firm, operates in more than forty countries and employs over 120,000 staff worldwide. The Capgemini University supports the Group's key initiatives through a global curriculum that spans classroom, on-site and online training, and delivers over one million learning hours each year in multiple locations.

In terms of resourcing, the university relies on a large team of facilitators to deliver high quality learning experiences. The Group's increasing need for learning support has led the university to adopt a more systematic approach to managing and enhancing the capabilities of its facilitator pool.

The facilitators are internal staff, with other day-jobs, so facilitation is something additional that they do. Although there is a tradition of internal facilitation within Capgemini, the university faced the same two key challenges that any business with internal facilitators faces: how to ensure consistent high quality and how to ensure access to their time.

To begin with, the university identified a pool of respected, experienced practitioners in different professional areas of expertise. To help ensure skill levels and drive consistency of quality, they designed a University Facilitator Competency Framework (UFCF), which describes eight dimensions of facilitator competency (see Figure 5.2).

This framework helps the university to distinguish between four facilitator competency levels:

1. Facilitator in Training (FIT): facilitators who join courses as part participants, part observers and part facilitators.
2. University Facilitator (UF): facilitators who deliver modules and provide inputs to course design/redesign under the guidance of a UQF.

FIGURE 5.2 Capgemini University Facilitator Competency Framework

3. University Qualified Facilitator (UQF): facilitators who lead course delivery, mentor and coach other facilitators, and contribute to course design and development.

4. University Faculty (UFa): UQFs who lead both learning and transformation programmes. They also play substantial roles in new course design and provide input for university strategy and key initiatives.

The framework does more than merely ensuring competency; it is also used to support development. The university has thus created a number of tools and platforms to support its facilitators in their professional development. There is an Onboarding Guide, a T-Book and a range of hints and tips videos to help facilitators develop new ways of delivering their content. The university has also worked to foster an active Facilitator Community using its internal social media platform and it runs sessions at every central delivery event so that facilitators can network on site.

The university's aim has not been only to develop a reliable resource but also to foster a loyal community of expertise. Top facilitators and their managers receive a personal thank you letter from the executive leader of their business unit every year and each successful facilitator is personally thanked by the university after each delivery.

The UFCF was launched in 2009 and currently has over 500 facilitators. The initiative has delivered four key benefits:

1. Consistency of delivered learning experience, irrespective of where the programme is delivered, which is vital as the university moves to more virtual and in-country delivery.
2. A strong community of facilitators who share best practices and experiences.
3. A clear development path for facilitators with a professional development framework, which is recognised and valued across the business.
4. Added value at the business level in accelerating capability development and time-to-market.

6 Demonstrating the value of corporate learning: answering the evaluation conundrum

Here's a conundrum for you. As previously mentioned, demonstrating the value of learning is *the* number one challenge reported by learning executives today.[121] Consistently, persistently, it tops the list of survey after survey. And yet, the same research also shows that at least three-quarters of organisations do not measure the impact of learning *on the business*.[122] In fact, a 2009 survey of Fortune 500 CEOs showed that while 96 per cent of executives wanted to see information on the business impact of learning initiatives, only 8 per cent were receiving it.[123] So on the one hand learning leaders report feeling acutely aware of the need to show the value of what they do, but on the other hand they do not appear to be doing anything about it. Or at least, not anything successful. It's as if we are stuck in a rut and unsure of how to get out of it. Which begs the questions of how did we get here in the first place, and what exactly do we have to do to get out?

What makes this situation particularly intriguing is that for most readers it is probably old news. Commentators were noting the inadequacy of learning evaluation over forty years ago[124] and not much has improved since then. Indeed, perhaps the bigger conundrum here is how we appear to have got away with not auditing what we do for so long. For despite our inability to prove value, organisations continue to invest billions of dollars on formal training and development programmes and probably a similar amount on informal initiatives, effectively on faith alone. It is hard to imagine any other area of business in which such significant and sustained investment would be matched with so little audit or follow-up for so long.

But things are changing. The world has turned, the economic and business environment is evolving, and the honeymoon is all but

over. Demand for proof of the impact and value of learning is growing fast, prompted by budgetary pressures and concern about the efficacy of learning interventions.[125] Expectations are changing, and the
challenge for many learning leaders is that, to retain their credibility
in business, they need to adapt and find ways to provide something
that for the past forty years has not been demanded of them in quite
the same way.

This chapter is about how learning leaders can meet this challenge. At the heart of demonstrating value lie two quite different
tasks – measuring impact and then reporting it – and I look at each
in turn. Much of what I focus on is the issue of measurement, since
this is the key cause of our lack of progress, and on the way things
may get a little technical. But please bear with me because the devil,
as is so often the case, is in the detail.

There are some who say that measuring the value of learning
is essentially a simple subject made unnecessarily complicated. I
disagree. I think it is in fact a very technical and complex subject
that has not yet been made sufficiently operationally simple. So
before we explore how corporate learning functions can best show
off the value of what they do, we need to take a look at some of
these complexities and what can be done about them. We will look
at why evaluation practice has not significantly improved over the
past half century, and at what exactly the challenges are and what
learning leaders can do to tackle them. First, though, let's step
back and check what evaluation currently goes on and answer the
initial conundrum of why there is so little evaluation of business
impact.

WHAT ARE BUSINESSES CURRENTLY DOING?

Despite the headline about the lack of impact evaluation, there is no
shortage of evaluation activity. A 2011 survey of HR professionals[126]
found that learning evaluation takes place in around 80 per cent of
respondents' organisations. There is evidence that it is most likely
to occur in larger organisations with a specific training budget, and

that it is more common in more developed countries and in the private sector.[127] Generally, though, most companies seem to be doing something.

The problems come when we look at *what* organisations are doing. Study after study across different countries and cultures has reported the same finding: post-course 'happy sheets' or 'smile sheets', which only evaluate what attendees think of the learning, are by far the most commonly used method of evaluation, and most evaluations do not go much further than this.[128] Estimates of the number of companies that assess business impact vary from 2 per cent[129] to 36 per cent,[130] although most seem to be around 10 to 15 per cent.[131]

So it is not that there is no activity, it is just that it is not the right activity. There are two main types of evaluation – *summative* and *formative*.[132] Summative evaluation is what mostly happens now: evaluation that provides feedback and other data to help improve learning programmes. What is largely missing is *formative* evaluation: evaluation that can assess outcomes and thereby help inform decision-making about learning. And by 'outcomes', I mean whether programmes deliver what they are supposed to, what impact they have on the business, and who gains most and least from them.

WHY IS SO LITTLE FORMATIVE EVALUATION BEING DONE?

The explanations put forward for why so little has been done for so long can be divided into two main camps: those concerning demand and those citing supply. On the demand side, commentators have questioned the historical levels of demand for evaluation and levelled the accusation that organisations have not genuinely cared about it, or at least have not seen it as a priority.[133] The fact that providers have not previously made more of an effort to demonstrate the value of their work also seems to support this notion of a lack of real demand. In this vein, it has been noted that many learning functions seem to have seen evaluation as a perfunctory task[134] and that by and large evaluations have not often been used to inform decision-making about organisational learning.[135]

The most obvious reason for this is that evaluation has not been seen as sufficiently useful to warrant prioritising it.[136] This could simply be because learning has intuitively been assumed to work and evidence of the specifics of how it has done so has not been deemed necessary.[137] An alternative reason is that from a purely behavioural economics viewpoint there have been few incentives for pursuing thorough evaluation. This, then, is the fear that 'learning doesn't work'[138] and the thorny issue of vested interests: that although everyone may have something to gain from a rigorous evaluation, almost everyone has something to lose, too.[139] It is in very few stakeholders' interests to find out that a learning programme has not been successful – with the exception of safety-related training. And there is nothing like the fear of what they might find to stop people looking.

A final possible reason for a historical lack of real demand is that evaluation is seen as ineffective. Given that the majority of evaluations appear to focus on whether attendees enjoyed themselves and thought highly of the venue, business leaders could be forgiven for feeling this way. Indeed, in light of the guidelines for training providers on how to achieve 'perfect' scores on happy sheets, which include tips like not letting people complete them on an empty stomach and the importance of having plush name cards, a degree of cynicism about some evaluations seems wise. For all the reasons suggested above, it does appear that traditionally the demand for evaluation has run only skin-deep.

On the supply side of the equation, explanations for the historical lack of impact evaluation centre on logistical challenges, in particular a lack of resources,[140] a lack of expertise and some big methodological issues. The resources that may be lacking are money and time;[141] support for this comes from the finding that the tendency not to evaluate fully is particularly high in small and medium-sized enterprises with fewer resources.[142] On the expertise front, commonly cited challenges are a lack of understanding about what needs to measured[143] and a lack of training in how to evaluate.[144] And on the methodological front, there is the continual issue of how to measure the impact of benefits when they are intangible and not directly tied to performance.[145] The results of these logistical challenges are that evaluation is often outsourced to the learning provider, and learning leaders are frustrated at not being more able to demonstrate the value of what they do. A recent survey, for example, found that 80 per cent of senior HR professionals believe that learning delivers more value to their organisation than they are able to demonstrate.[146]

MOVING FORWARD

Uncertain demand and concerns about the ability to supply appear to have limited the formative evaluation being undertaken. But expectations *are* changing and demand *is* developing. So learning leaders are going to have to address the supply challenges because continuing to engage in poor quality evaluations will only serve to undermine the credibility of both the evaluations and the learning. To overcome these issues and make some decisions about what can be done going forward, we first need to sort fact from opinion and to be clear about what evaluation can and cannot do. And to understand this, we need to take a brief look at the history of evaluation and at how it has evolved over the past half century.

A (very) brief history of evaluation

The history of evaluation in organisational settings can be seen as beginning in 1959. This was the year that Donald Kirkpatrick published a series of articles outlining his 'Hierarchical Model of Training Outcomes'[147] and, in the fifty years since, Kirkpatrick's model has become ubiquitous: the starting point for almost all discussions about how learning should be evaluated. And that's pretty much it – I said it would be brief.

Kirkpatrick's achievement

I could, I suppose, have mentioned a couple of the more enduring attempts to extend Kirkpatrick's theory and operationalise it with rigorous methodology, such as the emphasis on ROI (return on investment) that emerged in the 1990s, or the ROE (return on expectations) movement that has developed as attempts to measure ROI have faltered. But so ubiquitous is Kirkpatrick's theory that saying that the history of evaluation has – so far – begun and ended with him is not as big an exaggeration as one might think. Although this is testimony to how the model has helped move the field of evaluation forward, it is also evidence that the field has not succeeded in moving much beyond it.[148]

The success of the model lies in its apparent simplicity.[149] It describes four different types or levels of learning outcome:

- Level 1, *reactions*, is how participants feel about the learning event.
- Level 2, *learning*, is the knowledge or skills acquired during the learning.
- Level 3, *behaviour*, is the application of this learning on the job.
- Level 4, *results*, is the impact of the learnt and replicated behaviour on organisational targets.

Kirkpatrick described these levels as hierarchical, in that each level is assumed to have an impact on the next; so whether participants like the learning event (reactions) is assumed to have an impact on their inclination to study and learn, which in turn can drive behaviour and so forth.

The model is essentially a taxonomy or classification scheme,[150] and its single biggest contribution is that it created a common vocabulary to help focus discussions about evaluation.[151] Other people have suggested other categorisations. But whether because of first-mover advantage or for some other reason, Kirkpatrick's model has held sway. The sheer amount and intensity of debate that the model has stimulated is amazing. And through this debate, three key limitations of the model have emerged, which should be borne in mind when thinking about whether and how to do evaluation:[152] the oversimplification and incompleteness of the model, the untested presence of a cause–effect relationship between the different levels, and the unproven progressive importance of information at each level.

Limitation 1: a limited range

First, Kirkpatrick's model focuses overly on participant outcomes and the quality of the learning event at the expense of other very important factors. Indeed, the impact of learning has been shown to depend on a whole host of factors, of which the actual learning event is just one.[153] Probably the best example here is organisational climate or culture, which has been shown to be more important in determining whether learning has an impact on performance than the learning event itself.[154]

A number of suggestions have been made for ways to capture these various other variables into a simple model. Examples include the CIRO (context, input, reaction, outcome) model,[155] the CIPP (context, input, process, product) model[156] and the IPOO (input, process, output, outcome) model.[157] None has managed to challenge Kirkpatrick's model for dominance, though, possibly because they can sound – and sometimes are – more complicated. Yet many of these models do have merit and the original point remains: if you think only in terms of the elements of Kirkpatrick's model, you will miss looking at some critical factors that could significantly impact your learning efforts.

Limitation 2: liking does not produce learning

A second issue is that the model is generally understood to imply causal relationships between the levels. So, for example, positive reactions to the training are seen as helping create learning, and learning is in turn seen as a determinant of subsequent behaviour changes.[158] All of which sounds intuitively reasonable and logical. The problem, though, is that studies fail to support this.[159]

For instance, there is evidence that reactions are important for ensuring interest, attention and motivation to learn. And there can be little doubt that if participants hate a learning event it is usually doomed by its poor reputation alone. But although good reactions may be necessary for success, as sources of data about business impact they appear to be pretty useless. Repeated research has shown that measures of *affective reactions* (how pleased participants are with the learning event), such as happy sheets, bear almost no relationship to whether participants will change their behaviour back in the workplace.[160] Similarly, and perhaps more surprisingly, it appears that tests of learning at the end of an event do not help predict subsequent performance in the job.[161] Indeed, simply asking someone at the end of a learning event if they think the learning is going to be useful (called *utility reactions*) is just as predictive of later job performance as testing what they have learned.[162]

Moreover, a subtler, more insidious issue here is that a singular or overly strong emphasis on participant reactions can inadvertently create significant cultural challenges.[163] For example, it can create expectations that training must be entertaining, with the consequence that trainers may emphasise participant enjoyment rather than learning. In addition, it can reinforce the all-too-common perception that it is the trainer's responsibility to ensure that participant learning occurs.

The relevance of this for organisations lies in the prevalence of evaluations that focus on level 1, reactions, often with the implied premise that 'it may not be perfect, but it's better than nothing'. Well, it may be better than doing *absolutely* nothing, but the research shows that what it does is a lot closer to nothing than many people assume. Interestingly, the magnitude of the relationship between learning reactions and learning impact appears to be roughly the same as the typical relationship between job satisfaction and job performance.[164] And yet organisations that would (quite rightly) deride the thought of replacing annual appraisals with job satisfaction measures seem perfectly happy with measuring the impact of multi-million pound learning programmes with a similarly effective measure.

These issues have not fallen on deaf ears, though; they have led many researchers and practitioners to try to explore various methods for assessing level 4, business impact – or results. This leads us to the third major limitation of the model.

Limitation 3: the ROI obsession

This issue is more philosophical and, to be fair to Kirkpatrick, it's not all the fault of his model. Built deep into the model, though, is the idea that the further up the levels one goes (i.e. the closer to level 4), the better the evaluation will be. It is this logic that has at least partly fuelled an obsession among some people for measuring the financial impact of learning – its ROI. Analyses of learning ROI can be traced to the 1950s, but it was not until the early 1980s that the term 'ROI' was used explicitly in learning evaluations. Early research focused on whether training could improve company performance, and out of these early studies came some impressively lengthy and detailed discussions about how best to calculate ROI. These calculations are sometimes described as operationalising Kirkpatrick's fourth level, and at other times as providing a new, fifth level. Probably the most famous example is the work of Phillips,[165] who suggested some excellent general guidelines about how organisations could identify ROI. From all that has been written some seductively simple looking formulae have emerged, too, such as:

$$\text{ROI} = (\text{total benefit} - \text{total cost}) \,/\, \text{total cost} \times 100\%$$

Yet for all their innocent appearance, formulae such as these can hide some devilishly intricate calculations and methodological difficulties that are notoriously hard to deal with. Not least of these is the tricky issue that a lot of learning activity produces benefits such as employee satisfaction that are almost impossible to translate into dollar values (which you need to do in order to calculate an ROI). Or how do you calculate opportunity cost (the cost of not doing what you would be doing if you weren't attending a learning event)? And then, of course, there is the issue that when you really look at it, there are a surprisingly large number of variables involved, all of which should strictly speaking be accounted for in your formula. To address these challenges, researchers have developed elaborate and complex equations to try to capture all the variables. Yet despite this, the challenges involved eventually lead to guesses or assumptions about the dollar values of factors, which seems to undermine the whole point of engaging in something as rigorous as an ROI study.

Yet ROI has persisted as an object of desire. When asked what they would evaluate, if they could, most survey respondents put ROI close to the top of their list.[166] Indeed, some researchers suggest that it is desirable to go even further and try to measure societal impact,[167] though why organisations would want to do this is not always clear. The harsh reality is that although it remains an ideal for many, the methodological complexities and sheer mathematics of calculating ROI are simply beyond most HR professionals and business leaders alike.[168]

Moreover, to return to the original issue, the focus on ROI often carries with it an implied assertion that it is the highest form of evaluation. And on paper, it may be. But in the context of an organisational setting, it isn't always so. I admire the work of Phillips and believe that measuring ROI is an excellent idea that is sometimes possible. However, I also believe that ROI is only one way of measuring business impact, that it can have significant methodological challenges, and that it is not necessarily always the best, most appropriate or most value-adding approach. As many commentators have pointed out, not all learning warrants – in pure financial terms if nothing else – the time and money required to do a full ROI study.[169] More, it seems, is not always better.

There is a subtler risk here, too. The idea that harder financial-impact data is better can create pressure for learning functions and providers to generate evaluation data that looks rigorous and hard and financially relevant. And in trying to achieve this they can end up presenting data as something that it is not, which risks generating cynicism and undermining the credibility of the learning function.

Along these lines, one of the more dangerous trends at present in my view is the idea of *return on expectations* (ROE). This is an idea that has been promoted by the Kirkpatrick camp among others as a potential solution to the difficulties with assessing ROI. On the one hand, I entirely agree with the sentiment of checking if the business expectations of learning programmes are met. On the other hand, I am aware that the idea is open to poor application. Phillips,[170] for instance, cites the wonderful example of a business reporting that a programme had an impressive 85.2 per cent ROE and presenting this as data that reflected the impact of the programme, yet the calculations were based on simply asking participants whether their expectations were met. Therefore, although the sentiment behind it is admirable and there are some excellent examples of well-implemented ROE evaluations, I nonetheless believe that ROE is a dangerous concept because it can mean whatever you want it to and is thus particularly open to misguided application.

It's not as easy as it looks

It is clear that despite the ubiquity of Kirkpatrick's model of *what* to evaluate, there is no consensus on *how* best to evaluate. Part of the reason for this is that, with the exception of a few easily measured learning objectives, evaluating business impact is fraught with methodological difficulties. To make informed decisions about what to do going forward, it is important to clearly understand what these key methodological challenges are. And two major ones need to be highlighted.

The first methodological challenge is the 'criterion issue':[171] how can you be sure when change happens? With knowledge, it is easy – you can test it before and after. And there are some directly performance-related skills, such as sales ability, that are also easy to measure. But with much behaviour it is more difficult. Self-report measures are notoriously unreliable, since participants have a tendency to underestimate their pre-learning ability and overestimate their post-learning ability.[172] And despite the popularity of 360-degree feedback – in particular to assess the impact of coaching – feedback from others is not much better, since feedback givers are prone to overrate and to change how they rate as their expectations of a person change.[173] There is some evidence that asking individuals to rate the degree of change is more effective than pre- and post-tests,[174] but these are still not perfect. Annual performance ratings are also often used, but with such global, unspecific measures it is not clear whether any change in the ratings is due to the skills or behaviour that the learning targeted. So knowing when things have genuinely changed is not easy.

The second issue is how to isolate the effect of a learning event. Assuming you find an improvement in performance, how do you calculate what proportion of it is due to the learning? Even for workers whose output can be easily measured, such as sales people, there are often simply too many other factors involved to prove clearly that an improvement in performance is only the result of training. This does not mean that such data cannot be used, but it does mean that all data points need to be used carefully and with a questioning mindset. The classical way of approaching this issue is to use control groups – to have two groups of people as similar as possible in every way and to put only one of the groups through the learning event. However, this is usually not feasible within an organisational setting, so there are few examples of the use of control groups. And even if you do manage to achieve this, you still have the 'Hawthorne effect' to account for,[175] in which merely observing people can effect changes in their performance levels, plus the fact that the economic and business environment itself can emphasise or hide the impact of learning on organisational performance levels.[176] So even when you do find change, knowing where it has come from is not easy.

Put together, these two challenges mean that there are many areas of learning in which demonstrating change and thereby business impact requires an act of faith in your figures, a faith that many researchers feel uncomfortable with, but that most learning leaders have little choice but to accept. Indeed, a critical point here is that evaluations do not have to be technically perfect. They do not always have to ensure that they isolate the impact of learning alone and unequivocally demonstrate impact on the bottom line. But they do need to show in a credible fashion the degree to which learning impacts on things that the business cares about. This brings us to *how*.

PRINCIPLES FOR ACTION

I began this chapter by stating that I believe evaluation is a complicated subject that has not yet been made operationally simple enough. Hopefully I have demonstrated why I believe it to be a complicated subject technically and methodologically. When these complexities are oversimplified in models and methods, or not acknowledged or addressed, poor quality evaluations are the inevitable result. This is hugely detrimental because if learning leaders are to gain the respect of business leaders, they have to use credible numbers in a credible fashion. Yet there appears to be a gulf between much of the research that exists and what is being practised on the organisational frontline. Translating the complexities of the research findings into simple, easily implementable practice remains to be achieved.

There is a degree to which this is mission impossible. It is not useful, for example, to simply suggest that a particular type of evaluation should always be used with a specific type of learning because the best method of evaluation to use will be specific to the situation. But although I see the emergence of a compellingly simple model that simultaneously captures all the complexities of evaluation as unlikely, I do believe that simple guidelines are possible. As a step in this direction, I offer six key principles that I believe should guide all decision-making about when and how to do evaluation.

Commit to evaluate impact

In these days of corporate cutbacks, lean structures and shareholder accountability, I believe that there is nothing short of an ethical responsibility to assess the impact of learning. We simply cannot continue to invest so many resources into learning without having such accountability. Or at least we cannot continue to invest without accountability and expect to retain our credibility as a professional body. Moreover, at a fundamental level, without evaluation, corporate learning risks descending into mediocrity and irrelevance. Learning is a market and if we want quality, efficacy and efficiency to prevail, we need to apply market pressures. We need to be able to make informed judgements. And for that, we need to evaluate business impact.

This doesn't, by the way, mean that you should no longer use happy sheets. They still have an important role to play in helping to improve the quality of learning initiatives. But the first principle is simple: commit to evaluate, and not just using happy sheets. Commit to evaluate the business impact of learning initiatives. One caveat is that collecting data for data's sake is pointless. Small, one-off learning investments may not warrant evaluation, for instance. But as a rule of thumb, if it is possible to evaluate the impact of something, you should do so.

In terms of what counts as measuring impact, it can mean ROI, but equally valid data may be sales numbers, safety rates or employee turnover. Remember: evaluations do not always have to directly show impact on bottom line performance – they just need to show how learning has affected performance-related targets that the business cares about. Importantly, though, we're talking about quantitative data here – numbers and figures. Merely collecting responses to the question 'How has this programme impacted your performance' and then selecting a few to show the business does not count as evaluating business impact. As for how to determine *what* to measure, well that leads us to the next principle.

Agree in advance with the business which measures to use

So how does one work out what the business cares about? Well, the fundamental purpose of evaluation is to determine the value of learning. Value, however, is a relative term, in that what is of great value to one organisational stakeholder may be of little value to another.[177] So in working out what to evaluate, an important first step is to know your audience – the customers and stakeholders of the programme – and to be realistic about what they want and need to know. This needs to be pitched right, too, for even by talking in technical terms such as levels of evaluation, learning professionals may risk confusing matters rather than clarifying them and be seen as not directly addressing the issues that matter most to business leaders.

Engaging your audience and involving them in identifying metrics is critical in ensuring the credibility of the evaluation and shared ownership of the success of the programme. The *how* of this can be straightforward, but it is almost impossible to rectify retrospectively if overlooked. Simply put, the process of evaluation must move from being a post-programme activity to an integral part of the design process and it must begin with determining learning needs and the crafting and contracting of learning objectives with the business. Indeed, in my experience, upfront clarity about what is to be achieved is often as effective as evaluation after the event. This is particularly so at more senior levels of organisations, where there is greater focus on knowledge workers and management, since the learning outcomes at this level tend to be more intangible and less directly related to immediate performance indicators.

Use measures linked to business objectives

This is a simple, but critical point: wherever possible the outcomes being measured should be linked to key business objectives. Where these outcomes are directly performance-related and specific to business units, the business-relevant objectives are likely to be reasonably clear. However, with cross-divisional leadership development programmes where the objective is to improve the overall effectiveness of individuals or teams, to disseminate common values and behaviours, or to ensure a flow of mobile and promotable talent, knowing what to evaluate is likely to involve less obvious and more indirect measures. The issue can be particularly complicated in global businesses where the very definition of value may vary between geographies and business units.

One question that can help determine what to evaluate is what, strategically, you want to achieve with the evaluation besides just proving the worth of learning. For example, with individuals on a programme for rising stars, you may wish to emphasise individual accountability for making the most of learning investments, and so track who tends to improve and who doesn't over the course of multiple interventions. Alternatively, you may wish to emphasise the role of managers in supporting and reinforcing learning initiatives, in which case you should develop measures to assess this. The measures may not be perfect, but purely by shining a light on certain issues you can draw attention to them and so change behaviour. As the old adage says, 'What gets measured gets valued'.

A recent example comes to mind of a large global financial services organisation that was frustrated by the lack of impact of repeated training initiatives aimed at improving the quality of performance management conversations. It was convinced by the quality of the training, received excellent happy-sheet feedback, and even had evidence of some immediate improvements in the quality of conversations back in the workplace. But every few years, it found itself back where it started. It was only when it evaluated the whole learning-to-performance process that it realised that the issue was as much about the organisational culture that learning attendees returned to as about individual capability. They were thus able to work towards moving away from the business treating learning as 'a sausage machine' and to help business leaders see it instead as a culture change initiative that they themselves needed to lead.

One consequence of this principle is that you should adapt your measures to each learning initiative. This may seem obvious, but researchers have noted that some evaluators always evaluate from a particular perspective such as ROI, rather than flexing their approach to meet situational demands. Undertaking an ROI study on a safety course, for instance, would be clearly unnecessary and arguably of dubious morality. You should always, then, be clear about the value proposition of your evaluation. Other than don't *just* use happy sheets and don't be constrained by Kirkpatrick's model, there are no simple rules here. It is important to be clear about the demands of each situation and how you are addressing them, rather than simply pursuing a familiar or favourite methodology.

Keep it simple and use existing metrics if possible

When it comes to data, less is more. By keeping your metrics few and simple, you can avoid creating an industry out of evaluation. The basic methodology can also be simple: make sure to establish baseline measures that can tell you the state of play before the learning (e.g. the average performance rating or output measure before learning) and then check them again after the learning. Moreover, by far and away the most successful method for evaluating impact is to use existing business metrics wherever possible.

To take the earlier example of the large financial services organisation that was trying to improve performance management conversations, it was alerted to the need for the learning by responses to specific questions in the employee opinion survey (only 43 per cent of respondents reported that their last appraisal conversation had helped them improve their performance). In this scenario, no ROI study was required and the business was able to use the pre-existing annual employee engagement study to evaluate impact. Purists may argue – quite rightly – that this did not isolate the impact of learning, nor show the effect on bottom line financial figures. However, from an organisational perspective the survey results were the impetus for learning, and what the business cared about was employees' perceptions of the utility of appraisal conversations, so the survey results were sufficient as evaluation measures.

Plan ahead to use your data

How evaluation data is used is often the most overlooked aspect of evaluation. At a basic level, it is critical to be clear about what you want to use the evaluation data for, about how and when you want to present the data to the business. What is even more critical, however, is to be clear about this *before* you begin the evaluation.

For example, I have frequently observed businesses in which different learning programmes have each been evaluated in different ways, collecting entirely different types of data. Clearly, distinctions between programmes will necessitate variations in how they are evaluated. But designing learning evaluations focused fully on the programme at hand, and only afterwards deciding how to incorporate various bits of evaluation data into a coherent report (assuming this is done at all), significantly restricts what you can do with the information. If the task is approached top-down, with end reporting by the corporate learning function in mind, there are likely to be common data points that can be collected. These can include three basic types of information:

- Operational data such as the number of participants, the cost per participant or the average utilisation of places available.
- Feedback data such as participant ratings of the learning.
- Impact data such as line manager ratings of impact, performance improvement figures or standardised impact ratings (e.g. a 1-to-10 scale based on the degree to which the agreed impact measures for each particular programme are achieved).

Whatever measures you use, it is important to consider at the start how you will integrate evaluation data from different programmes to provide an overall picture so you can be clear on what data you need to collect.

Own the evaluation, but share the work

Evaluation is complicated by vested interests, not least those of any external providers delivering the learning. No matter how positive your relationship with such providers, effectively outsourcing the evaluation to them is not wise. The organisation should always own the evaluation and be in charge of what it is measuring and how. Having said this, the workload can be shared. Although formative evaluation data must always be collected by the business itself, an external provider can be tasked with collecting summative evaluation data about the programme, such as immediate feedback, attendees and – to some degree – costs.

Identifying a good evaluation

Nine questions to ask when you consider an evaluation plan

1. How does it evaluate business impact? With which stakeholders have these measures been agreed?
2. How will you know when change happens? To what extent will you know that the learning programme is responsible?
3. How will the evaluation help ensure the continued improvement of the learning programme/event?
4. What will you be able to use the evaluation outputs for? How?
5. How does the evaluation data being collected for this programme/event align with data being collected for other programmes/events you are running?
6. How many data points are you collecting? How will this happen? How much time and money will it cost?
7. Who is collecting the data and who will be analysing it?
8. What is the plan for using and presenting the evaluation outcomes?
9. What will be the value of this evaluation to the business?

The six principles described above may not have the compact simplicity of Kirkpatrick's model, but hopefully they do begin to show some of the complexity involved and some of the key decision points that must not be overlooked if learning leaders are to adapt to the growing demands being placed upon them and produce evaluations that can truly demonstrate the value of what they do. As a subject and area of technical expertise, evaluation is complex and, at times, confusing. In implementation, though, it need not be so. In fact, in most cases it is perfectly possible to do it both easily and cheaply. The first step, and the objective of these principles, is to create a culture of evaluation, in which evaluation is viewed as an integral part of learning, and in which the business expects it to add value in its own right by ensuring that strategic decision-making about learning is informed by evidence. Yet measuring the impact and value of learning is of course just half the story. You may have proved its value to your own satisfaction, but doing so to an organisation's satisfaction can be an entirely different matter. So let us now look at the other part of this story: how best to present and use the data you gather through evaluations and other means.

REPORTING CORPORATE LEARNING

If evaluation is the science of demonstrating the value of corporate learning, then reporting is the art of it. Undoubtedly a skill in its own right, it is one that in my experience many corporate learning functions have yet to master. Indeed, compared to evaluation, reporting is an almost neglected subject. To be fair, some of this may well be down to the historical paucity and poor quality of data about learning that has been available. After all, if you struggle to get data, how to use it is less of a concern. But with the advent of LMSs capable of producing veritable reams of data, corporate learning functions increasingly have some real data to work with. Thus how to best use and report this data is fast becoming a hot topic.

There is more, and there is better

The traditional, most common way of reporting on learning has been through the use of regular (monthly or quarterly) dashboards, most often to highlight a few key data points: for example, financial, operational and feedback (happy sheet) data.

With access to such data becoming increasingly easy and efficient, many organisations have begun to step beyond dashboards and to replace or supplement them with bigger and more detailed reports. Yet more is not always better, and these more substantial reporting mechanisms have brought two big challenges. First, the sheer quantity of data available through LMSs is making knowing

what to present and – critically – what *not* to present more difficult. Second, LMSs' capability to gather operational data coupled
with the continuing lack of business impact data has tended to
give these reports a strong process bias (e.g. attendance rates, venue
costs). The danger in both these challenges is that well-intentioned
reporting mechanisms can become overwhelmed with operational
data that is of limited utility to the business, can appear to be data
gathering for data gathering's sake, and so may do little to help the
learning function's credibility or inform strategic decision-making
about learning.

Yet when supplemented with business impact data and properly presented, learning-related data can be a critical foundation of
the corporate learning function's standing within the business, its
passport to the decision-making table, and critical in helping to create a more informed and strategic approach to learning across the
business. So how best can this data be reported? Well, as ever, opinions differ, and what is best depends on your business and its culture. But some clear guidelines do rise above the debate.

Establish regular reporting mechanisms
If you don't already have them, establish regular reporting mechanisms – I recommend either biannually or annually for major reports
and perhaps quarterly for briefer update reports. The key here is to
be in sync with your business's rhythm. An interesting effort in this
regard can be seen in the Talent Development Reporting Principles
(TDRP) initiative recently launched in the United States. This is
a collaborative attempt by several independent learning leaders to
develop common reporting standards and consistently defined measures that can be presented in regular business statements, which
summarise the impact of talent, learning and development initiatives. They identify different kinds of reports and suggest different
timelines for them: for example, monthly operational reports and
quarterly summary reports in addition to a more complete annual
report.

Have different reports for different purposes and different audiences

Not everyone needs to see all the data. So, as implied above, consider different reports for different purposes and people. For example, the TDRP initiative suggests designing these various reports according to the kinds of information the audiences need and the level of detail they will tolerate. Thus, it recommends limiting access to detailed monthly programme and operational reports to within the learning function, whereas it views brief summary reports or dashboards as a good way to provide updates for business leaders, and recommends tailoring the content accordingly.

With this in mind, I recommend that if you do use Kirkpatrick's model as a guide, level 1 data (reactions) should by and large only be used for internal corporate learning function reports, and level 2 and 3 data (learning and behaviour, respectively) should be used only very sparingly in business reports, and then only when knowledge or skill acquisition is a key target of the learning programme (e.g. product training courses).

Happy-sheet data should not be included in reports for the wider business. The only caveat is that some companies have noted the utility of presenting data on Net Promoter Scores to their business stakeholders: i.e. responses to the question, 'How likely is it that you would recommend this [learning initiative] to a colleague?' Beyond this, though, happy-sheet scores should be kept within the function.

Report only what you need to

One common mistake that I see in Learning Reports is that everything is included. Yet the sheer size of these reports can be as dispiriting as they are impressive, and can make it difficult for readers to quickly identify what is important. One way to ensure that your reports do not disappear under the weight of detailed data is to focus on major issues, for example organising your annual report around the annual strategic learning objectives agreed with the business. Don't be overwhelmed by including every single programme – think more about what's important to your business leaders and has been agreed with them and highlight those areas. If you really do feel the need to include the detail, for example if your business culture values such detail, put it in an appendix. Simply put, the briefer the report, the better.

Provide some context

Try to avoid presenting just bland data – how many people attended, where from and how many people completed. Without some context, straightforward numbers like these can be meaningless for the reader. Aim to help the reader grasp the 'so what' of these numbers. One easy way to do this is to present your data with comparison points, such as trend figures (how they compare with the previous report's numbers), benchmark data (how they compare with other learning initiatives) and target data (how they compare with objectives).

Have an end in mind

There are two core reasons to report corporate learning data. The first is simple accountability. You are investing the organisation's money and need to be able to show what you are doing with this investment. The second is, in one way or another, to inform decision-making (usually about learning). So it is to report and inform, though of course when I say 'inform' I assume that there is an objective in mind – something that the CLO wishes to achieve with this data, be it extra funding, a change in policy, or even a discussion about how learning is being done and to what end.

When developing a Corporate Learning Report, it is imperative to keep these basic functions in mind and to be clear what you wish to achieve with the report. This latter point is vital, because for any report to be meaningful and valuable, it needs to convey something that helps its audience understand what to do next. It should trigger an essential discussion or a decision to be made. Otherwise, the report risks just being glanced at before being filed away: a box ticked. Therefore, all reports – including programme and operational reports – should always have a concluding section in which the consequences of the data being reported are laid clear: e.g. whether you're meeting targets, what decisions need to be made and what your recommendations are.

Don't make an industry of it
As guidelines go, this one is simple but important. I have seen some corporate learning functions make an industry out of data reporting – putting unbelievable amounts of resources into producing reports that yield limited value. As a simple guideline, if developing the report feels like an all-consuming chore, you're probably doing too much.

Presentation is key
In a recent study by the Miami School of Business, researchers found that investors, regardless of their experience, place a higher value on firms with attractive annual reports than they do on those that produce less attractive reports. Presentation matters. However great your data is, if you don't present it well, it won't be received well. Make it look professional, and it has a chance of being deemed professional.

There are two important elements to consider here. The first is simple appearance – how it looks. The Miami researchers, for example, highlighted the positive impact of colour in particular. The second element is structure – ensuring the data in the report document is presented clearly and simply. One distinction that is often used here is that of efficiency data and efficacy data. Efficiency data concerns attendance numbers, costs and so forth, while efficacy data concerns the key business impact objectives, such as lowered staff turnover or improved sales figures. Thus efficiency data is useful for answering questions such as who are we investing in and how much? Efficacy data, meanwhile, is useful for answering questions such as what are we getting in return for this investment and are we meeting our objectives?

With this in mind, a standard basic structure for an annual or biannual report is:

- Executive summary, with clear headline findings, decision points and recommendations.

- Impact (efficacy) data, addressing each of your strategic learning objectives in turn and the business impact achieved.
- Operational (efficiency) data, such as participant information, completion rates for programmes and usage data for e-learning.
- Financial (efficiency) data, such as costs, learning investment per employee.
- Consequences and conclusions, including a summary of the past year's performance and recommendations for the future.

Reporting corporate learning

Questions to ask yourself when developing a reporting process

1. Who are your key audiences (e.g. internal learning function staff, key business stakeholders, board members)?
2. How frequently will you produce each report (e.g. your programme reports, operational reports and executive reports)?
3. Which bits of information are important for each of these audiences to receive? For example, when there are decision points, which audience group will make those decisions?
4. What is the purpose of each report and what is the intended value and objective of each one?
5. Have you communicated and agreed with the business how and when you will report?
6. For each type of report, have you laid out a simple, clear and consistent structure that is capable of delivering the report's objective?
7. Is numerical data always provided with some context to help aid its interpretation?
8. If the report is intended for a business audience, is it clear and concise?
9. How much time, effort and money will compiling reports require? Do the benefits that the reports will yield justify the investment?
10. Do you have the necessary design and presentation skills to ensure the reports look good and are easy to read?

CONCLUDING THOUGHTS

In 2004, an Accenture survey found that 16 per cent of learning functions produced an annual Learning Report. These days the figure has grown to closer to 30 per cent, but still only a minority of businesses produce such reports regularly. And those that are produced all too often consist of little more than lists of operational data and happy-sheet scores. For too long, in too many businesses, evaluation and reporting have been not much more than tick-box exercises or afterthoughts. The resulting documents are briefly presented before ending up in a desk drawer somewhere. Given their quality, this may well be the best place for them.

As a function, corporate learning can struggle with credibility when it comes to data, and ineffective evaluations and poor reporting merely serve to compound this. It is not only the damage being done by poor reporting that is a concern but also the opportunity being lost. If all we show the business is bland learning attendance figures, we will always be seen as an equally bland service function. Yet reporting provides us with an opportunity to do much more than this and gives us a platform to demonstrate our ability to impact business results and so earn our place at the strategic decision-making table.

Of course, there is a considerable risk in all this: by committing to evaluate the business impact of what we do, we need to make sure that we are having a business impact. This razor's edge is likely to cause some discomfort, but we cannot avoid it because our credibility and continued influence as a profession is at stake. And in the next chapter I look at this critical subject of credibility and reputation: the branding of the corporate learning function.

Case study: marketing and metrics at the Disney/ABC group

When Clare O'Brien joined the Disney/ABC Television Group in 2010 as Director of Learning and Development she found an amazingly diverse business, with seventeen separate business units. A variety of learning programmes were provided for employees, but take-up was patchy, as was their connection to performance reviews and business priorities.

Employee survey results showed a great desire for learning and development, as well as guidance on what programmes would help build capabilities for success. By engaging business leaders in developing a common learning strategy and with the enthusiastic support from senior executives, Clare created a radical plan. We say 'radical' because it was a fundamental departure from what existed before and utilised innovative applications, but it was built on some very solid foundations.

Working with the company's leaders to identify business priorities, she created five learning pathways, focused on topics such as leadership, business acumen and innovation. In doing so, she simplified the learning offering, making it more targeted and clearer for people to understand both the needs it was serving and what it was trying to achieve. Having looked across the market at generic learning offerings, Clare then made a key decision: to hire in some top learning professionals to create much of their content in-house. Which is exactly what they did: thirty-seven programmes in total, which they made available across multiple platforms. So far, so simple, but what Clare and her team did next is really interesting.

First, understanding that getting people to attend would be a key challenge, they developed a marketing strategy. This had three main elements. To engage business leaders and help ensure that people got time away from their work to attend learning, Clare and her team embarked on a long tour of roadshows, taking the new strategy to the business and explaining the improvements and benefits to them. They also developed a plan to make learning more accessible. They created bite-sized versions: brief content designed to be consumed by those with little time. And they created a simple, but slick, online interface between their LMS and employees, making it easier for people to see what learning was available and relevant to them, as well as making it simple to enrol. They then created a monthly electronic newsletter, sent to all employees, which informs them of new learning initiatives, lists the top-attended programmes, and presents the ratings and reviews that events have received from attendees. Importantly, this email also has quick links for course enrolment. Through these activities alone, Clare and her team delivered a 243 per cent increase in enrolment. But they went further.

Utilising Web 2.0 technology, they crowdsourced reviews, enabling and encouraging attendees to go online and rate and comment upon the programmes they attended. And just as with the crowdsourced reviews on Amazon.com, everyone gets to see the ratings and reviews posted. By introducing this system, they were not only engaging people in the process of learning, but were also creating a community atmosphere for it. That's not all, though, because just as with Amazon.com, people can see what courses other people are attending – along the lines of 'people who attended this programme also attended A, B and C ...' In doing so, they are effectively crowdsourcing developmental suggestions for people.

So Clare and her team hit upon some really interesting ways of using technology to market their learning products. What makes this case particularly interesting is that they combined this marketing strategy with a measurement one. So Clare hired in a metrics guru – someone to focus purely on collecting and leveraging data. They collect all the usual stuff: the numbers of people attending, the types of people attending, and their views about the relevance, utility and impact of the learning. But what really stands out is how Clare and her team use the data they collect to understand the learning behaviour and motivations of the customers they serve. On a simple level, they observe website behaviour – which links people click on and which resources they choose to use. But they also collect data on how people choose to learn (which platforms they use), how they go about enrolling, and – importantly – why they enrol. So they are not just collecting the standard process data, but are actively seeking and then using data points to understand their customers better.

Most importantly of all, they are reporting this data back to the business through regular scorecards and updates. They are, then, using reporting for a strategic purpose: to help business leaders better understand the process of learning and the needs, motivations and behaviours of their people.

7 Branding corporate learning: eliciting desire and engagement

One day, walking through his cornfield, farmer Ray Kinsella hears a voice that whispers, 'If you build it, he will come', and he sees before him a vision of a grand baseball field. To cut a long story short, he builds the baseball pitch and someone does indeed come. Slotting in at number 39 on the American Film Institute's all-time top 100 movie quotes, this famous saying from the film *Field of Dreams* may seem far removed from the world of corporate learning, but as has often been noted, it is a pretty accurate picture of most corporate learning functions' approach to marketing and branding. We build it and tend to assume that if we build it well enough, people will value it and seek our services. Or at least, that's what we've done historically. Now, however, in the face of heightening demand to demonstrate the value of our work, we are increasingly having to focus on how we can more proactively manage our businesses' perceptions of what we do.

This is a very real need because, as we have seen in previous chapters, the learning profession generally has a fairly lousy image at present. And the effect of this poor image shows in the frustrations and concerns learning leaders frequently express: that they sometimes struggle to get the take-up they need for courses, that their budgets are always the first to be cut, and that others in the business assume that learning is only about training courses, without appreciating the broader impact of what they do.

Part of the solution to this image issue is undoubtedly to provide better quality learning, and in the previous chapters I have described the problems in this regard and how they can be resolved. But in the face of stiff competition from business schools and external providers who are proactively managing and investing in their brands, merely building better products may not be enough. Corporate learning functions are going to need to build better reputations and brands, too. And a good product does not always ensure a good and strong brand.

In this chapter, I explore the world of learning branding. I look at how corporate learning functions are using branding, what learning brands consist of, and at how you should and can go about developing one. First, though, let's step back and look at the basics: what exactly is a brand and why should you care?

WHAT IS A BRAND AND WHY SHOULD YOU CARE?

Since its introduction in marketing theory in the 1960s, the concept of branding has entered everyday language. It has also evolved. Early definitions of branding focused merely on the development of product names, logos and slogans. And when most people think of branding this is still mainly what they think of. Yet these days, branding is understood to be about far more than markings: it is a combination of the physical and functional attributes and the benefits, experiences and values associated with a product or service. It is, in essence, anything and everything that is associated with you and your products.

As Peter Drucker once noted, marketing and branding are not specialised activities, but the business as a whole as seen from the perspective of its end result: the customers' point of view. While evaluation is about determining the value of individual learning initiatives, branding is about the business's perception of the learning function as a whole. A learning brand thus consists of your customers' views of how learning happens, how it is supported and encouraged, and what it achieves and serves. A brand has been described as 'a promise delivered',[178] which underlines a critical element of every brand: all the glossy logos and slogans in the world will do you no good unless you have the product and service to match.[179] Far from being ethereal and 'fluffy', branding is as pragmatic and grounded a concept as you can get.

I sometimes hear learning leaders say that their function does not have a brand, but this does not mean that it does not exist, more that they are not aware of it. In fact, it is impossible not to have a brand because people always have opinions. They may not tell them to you and you may not be aware of them, but they do have them. Come what may, the rest of the organisation will form an opinion about the corporate learning function and its products and capabilities, and the value that it does or does not add.

Thus, since you are going to have a brand anyway, why leave it to chance? You might as well actively manage your brand and try to shape it so that it is what you want it to be. This argument is strengthened by the fact that a brand is not something passive: it can add value in its own right. Like all ideas, it can affect people's behaviour. With products, branding is primarily used to increase sales and improve customer loyalty:[180] in essence, a reversal of branding's origins. It may have begun with farmers and ranch owners communicating a clear message to others, which said 'Hands off, this is mine'; but today branding does the opposite, saying 'Hands on, this is for you'.[181] What about a learning brand, though: what can it do and achieve, and how can it be used?

HOW CORPORATE LEARNING FUNCTIONS USE BRANDING

One of the few pieces of research into how learning functions approach branding was conducted in 2008.[182] It found that only 15 per cent of learning functions had a formal marketing and branding plan and that 62 per cent allocate no budget to this activity at all. Little wonder, then, that some commentators have called marketing and branding one of the areas of greatest weakness in the management of corporate learning functions.[183]

In a recent conversation, a learning leader told me that in his mind learning branding was primarily about 'making things look pretty'. And there is no doubt that branding does involve making things look attractive. Apple's approach to product design is ample proof of this. Yet when we consider how the few learning functions that *do* actively engage in branding are using their brands, we see it is for more than good looks. Five main purposes stand out:

1. *To communicate the presence and scope of the learning function.* In most firms this does not extend much beyond logos or the use of consistent colour schemes. But even then, by presenting a clear and consistent face to the organisation, it helps clarify in people's minds the range of activities that the function performs. This is probably the most common use consciously made of a learning brand.

2. *To improve learning outcomes by increasing take-up and engagement in programmes.* Probably the most pertinent example of this can be found in e-learning and self-directed learning initiatives such as communities of practice. Having a positive brand image can be critical in helping such initiatives succeed,[184] since the success of the learning depends to a huge extent on the motivation and engagement of learners, and therefore on their ideas about the desirability of the learning product. Thus, many business schools offering distance and self-directed learning products are proactively working to enhance the brand associated with them in order to improve take-up and completion rates.

3. *To improve business involvement with and support of learning initiatives.* The learning leaders I meet often regret the challenge they face in getting business leaders to actively sponsor, support and participate in learning initiatives. A strong and desirable brand, however, can significantly ease these challenges. An example here is the branding associated with IBM's technical training programmes, which have such a reputation for quality that business leaders actively want to be associated with them and so are more ready and willing to invest time to support and participate in these programmes.

4. *To communicate and ensure clarity about the learning function's strategy and purpose.* If this is clear, it is easier to ensure the perceived alignment and consistency of the function's various programmes. A learning brand can facilitate an understanding of the purpose of learning activity and so provide a context within which its various offerings can be understood. For example, if your learning function has strong branding about driving technical excellence, people encountering your learning products for the first time will understand them in this context and assume that they are part of this drive.

5. *As a transformational tool capable of impacting how businesses use learning.* For example, a learning brand that emphasises performance improvement and sustained behaviour change will result in business leaders understanding and approaching learning in a different way than if the brand centres on the rapid acquisition of knowledge and skills. I worked with an operational business unit recently in which learning was viewed pretty much like a 'sausage machine': people attended and learning was expected to come out the other end. There was little understanding of the ongoing process required and the challenges involved in ensuring sustained behaviour change. This might have been sufficient if the unit's learning objectives were simple knowledge or skill acquisition, but it was trying to achieve a more fundamental change in 'how things are done around here'. Part of the solution was to change the learning function's brand from that of operational sausage machine to deliverer of sustained change, as part of a wider initiative to change how business leaders understood and tried to use learning.

So the strength of learning brands lies in the value-add that they can deliver through mechanisms such as these. If you are struggling with any of these issues, more proactive brand management could be what you need. Before we consider how best to go about it, let us first take a closer look at the various elements that contribute to your learning brand and the levers you have to influence it.

BRAND COMPONENTS

Brands are formed through the experiences that customers, stakeholders and observers have of a business and its products. Over the years, various models have been proposed describing the elements that make up this experience. According to classic branding theory, it consists of three essential elements: *brand promise, brand experience* and *brand marketing*. The expectations people have of the learning function and its products are the brand promise; the experiences they actually have (such as whether their expectations are met) are the brand experience; and the ways the learning function chooses to promote itself and its products is the brand marketing.

I now present a model specific to learning branding to help you understand how to shape your brand. Building on my work with companies to help develop their learning branding, I have identified six key levers that corporate learning functions can pull to shape the experiences people have with them and, thus, their learning brand. This is not an exhaustive list, of course, but in my experience these levers are the most common and powerful at learning leaders' disposal.

Strategy

Your strategy is, in essence, the formalisation of your brand promise: it expresses the promise in a series of statements about why your function exists, the type of value it can add, and the specific object-ives it has in the short, medium and long term. In other words, it is the promises that you make to the business about the role your function will play, the services it will offer, and the impact it will have. It is *the* critical lever you have to shape your brand promise and the expectations people have of your function, which provide the context for their brand experience. Two factors play a big part in the promise you are perceived to be making: how clearly aligned you are with broader business objectives, and how specific and performance-oriented you are in describing your strategy. It is not just *what* you say that is important here, but also *how* you say it.

Products

As any salesman will tell you, there is nothing like a good product. The hard reality for learning functions is this: do the products and services you provide deliver on the promises you make? Your cap-acity to shape your learning brand with your products depends on more than only whether you deliver, though. The range, type and quality of your products, including the behaviours that they seek to change, the pedagogies that they use, and the delivery technologies that they employ, all form a key element of your brand experience. The key message here is that if you wish to reinforce your brand through the products you offer, they should produce the results you have promised *and* be consistent with the brand in their design and delivery. A short, focused product portfolio can be effective to communicate a clear sense of 'this is what we are about', whereas a broader product range is more likely to communicate a sense of a one-stop shop for all learning needs. In a similar vein, if your brand promise is all about enabling innovation, your products should not only focus on innovation but also live and breathe it through the pedagogies and technologies that they use.

Looks

Peter Cavanaugh, Head of Operations at General Electric's corporate university in Crotonville, relates how, when GE recently realigned and rebranded the Crotonville Centre, they looked at the walls and asked themselves, 'Is GE really beige?' Tangible features such as learning materials, marketing materials and, yes, even wall colourings can all communicate something about the intangible features of your learning brand. Glossy, professional materials convey something entirely different from less polished materials. So to some extent this is the 'making it look pretty' point, but it is more than this.

The norm for most corporate learning functions thinking about look is not to go much beyond trying to make things look good and perhaps aligning colour schemes with those of the broader business. Yet some organisations are doing more and deliberately use the look and feel of their learning products to reinforce both their learning brand and the broader business brand. McDonald's Hamburger University, for instance, purposefully mirrors and reinforces the broader business brand through a simple, clean design and the use of fun game-based learning tools. Likewise, media conglomerate Sky's online onboarding portal seeks to ensure that all new employees have a learning experience that's as much about aligning them with the Sky brand as about induction and gaining product knowledge. In practical terms, this is achieved through the tone of visuals, the style of the interactions, and the use of Sky video footage. So as well as exuding quality, looks can do far more.

Names

'What's in a name?' So asks Juliet of Romeo in Shakespeare's great masterpiece, before adding, 'That which we call a rose by any other name would smell as sweet.' Well, call me unromantic, but I am not entirely convinced. For sure, if your product is poor, then all the fanfare and glossy materials in the world can only hide that fact for so long. But as any marketing leader will tell you, names *do* matter, because they can communicate something about who you are, what you do and what you offer. They don't always, of course. There are examples of learning organisations in which the names of either the learning function or its component units are obscure and give little indication of what they really do. In my experience this is often the result of a lack of strategic clarity within the learning function and it represents both a missed opportunity and a problem, since the lack of clarity may impair the function's brand.

So what should you call yourself? One thing to state clearly here is that you should not feel compelled to call your function anything 'fancy'. The simple option is to adopt 'Learning' preceded by the company name, as in Novartis Learning, for example. Probably the most common alternative is to call the learning function a university. The practice began in the 1980s, as the 'university' brand was felt to add prestige to learning functions and to carry connotations of intellectual rigour.[185] Motorola's Corporate University, established in 1981, was one of the first examples of this new trend. The practice really took off and became commonplace in the 1990s, although it initially remained a largely US-based phenomenon. European countries were generally more protective of the term 'university' and so organisations there were slower to adopt it. The Capgemini University, founded in 1989, was a notable exception, but otherwise it was not until the late 1990s that the term became increasingly used outside the United States.

Yet for some in the corporate world, the term 'university' may also have negative connotations of an academic ivory tower, detached from reality and people. This was precisely Nike's concern when it decided to call its learning organisation NikeU rather than university. Of course, McDonald's reached the opposite decision with its Hamburger University, but made sure to balance this with a look and feel that is not at all 'ivory tower'.

Some companies have preferred other names with academic resonance, but which suggest something more focused in scope, such as the Allianz Management Institute and the Swiss Re Leadership Academy. The term 'business school' is rarely used, although Crédit Suisse has been successful with this name thanks to the fact that it has a dedicated building and runs a substantial operation. Whatever name you choose, though, care should be taken in choosing it. Calling yourself a university if your function is very small will do nothing for your credibility. The name you choose should communicate something clear about you and do so deliberately.

Places

If looks and names matter, it should be no surprise that places and locations do as well. Corporate reality experts have known for some time that buildings can contribute to the visual identity of an organisation by communicating something about its quality, principles and approach.[186] Seeking to capitalise on this, companies such as Capgemini and Banco Santander have invested in prestigious central learning facilities that have been decisive and deliberate elements in the construction of an equally prestigious brand for the learning function.

These central facilities also play a strategic role, providing a highly symbolic and important locus for unity in what, due to the sheer size of the companies, are otherwise dispersed learning functions. In this vein, Banco Santander's Solaruco complex within the Financial City outside Madrid is designed as a centre of identity. The name Solaruco, which refers to the place where the company originated, carries a strong emotional charge and serves as a reminder of the historical and cultural continuity of the Santander brand in a company that has embarked upon an aggressive agenda of international expansion.

Indeed, some locations become so iconic that they can generate reputations and sub-brands all of their own. Probably the best exemplar of this is the 'Pit', the amphitheatre-style classroom in which generations of GE's leaders have taught and learnt in its 53-acre campus in rural Crotonville, New York. Other examples include Daimler's Haus Lemmerbuckel outside Stuttgart, which has hosted learning activities for the Daimler group for decades; and Unilever's Four Acres property in London, along with its newer branch in Asia – Four Acres Singapore. The recent downturn triggered suggestions that such large complexes would become a thing of the past, yet this does not appear to have happened. A case in point here is the French multinational defence company Safran: after years of leasing the chateau at the Domaine de Béhoust outside Paris for its management training, it decided to acquire its own facility to make sure that it is branded and tied to the company.

Not all big organisations have or need such premises, of course: Barclays, Shell and BP operate successfully without them, promoting learning through regional units that coordinate the roll-out of locally delivered programmes, often in hired venues. Without a central facility, your choice of venue matters. Some years ago, in the name of cost consciousness, the learning function of one of the world's largest banks arranged to hold its most senior level leadership development programme in relatively budget accommodation next to the city zoo. After four days of poor food and sunrise 'wake-up calls' from the zoo's collection of chimps and howler monkeys, participants were less than thrilled. It was an experience that none of them forgot in a hurry, but not one that contributed positively to their experience of the learning programme or their opinion of the learning function staff. Needless to say, the location of the next programme was hastily shifted to one of the city's most prestigious hotels.

Of course, expensive is not always better, and even when locations have been carefully chosen, the impression they make is not always as intended. A few years back, a growing leadership consultancy invested heavily in a new building. Aware of research showing that location is more important for branding than the type of building, they made sure to choose an exclusive area.[187] In addition, cognisant of other research showing that the architecture of a building can have an effect on the interactions between the people in it, they chose an open-plan design with lots of informal meeting places and glass walls, to encourage interactions and idea sharing and reinforce their core values of openness and team working. And to be fair, the building achieved all these things. What they hadn't banked on, however, was many clients' reaction as they crossed the threshold: 'So this is what our (high) fees are paying for.' As with naming, location can be a powerful lever for branding, but it also needs to be carefully considered.

Behaviours

The final lever for shaping corporate branding is the all too often overlooked element of the behaviour of the learning function staff. Although corporate learning functions have products, to a large extent the functions are service businesses and, as with all such businesses, their employees are the main interface between the brand and their customers. Staff behaviour can thus have a powerful impact on customers' perceptions of the brand, and in this respect the branding can be seen as beginning with resourcing.

This fact is generally acknowledged, in that most if not all learning functions place great emphasis on the quality and credibility of their staff. Less considered, however, is that it is not only their level of expertise and the speed and quality of the service they offer that impacts the learning brand, but also the types of service they offer and the types of behaviour they demonstrate. For example, David Maister, in his book *The Trusted Advisor*,[188] distinguishes between four different types of relationship or service provided by professional advisors, each is associated with different behaviours.

- *Service offering-based advisors* tend to be subject matter or process experts who perform specific tasks usually focused on delivering solutions. A good example of this would be organising learning course logistics – particularly common in learning functions that outsource a lot of learning delivery.
- *Needs-based advisors* are subject matter experts who are a bit more like traditional consultants in that they become involved earlier on in the process and first help define needs and problems and then identify potential solutions.
- *Relationship-based advisors* perform much the same tasks as needs-based advisors, but whereas the latter tend to do so at the request of the business, the former do so proactively and are usually able to provide perspective beyond their area of technical expertise.
- *Trust-based advisors* are the pinnacle: they are entrusted with more information, involved in a broader range of activities and accepted as a core part of the business's leadership team.

For many corporate learning functions, some of their people are service offering-based advisors, involved in administration, while their 'learning managers' tend primarily to operate as needs-based or relationship-based advisors. Few reach the status of trust-based advisors. For Maister, the key to progressing to 'trusted advisor' status is what he calls the trust equation:

$$\text{Trust} = \frac{(\text{Credibility} \times \text{Reliability} \times \text{Intimacy})}{\text{Self-orientation}}$$

In this equation, the factors are:

- Credibility: expertise, presence and perceived honesty.
- Reliability: perceived dependability and consistency.
- Intimacy: perceived openness, not necessarily just with regard to private life, but with difficult issues and the range of topics seen as acceptable.
- Self-orientation: perceived preoccupation with own agenda.

The key is to be conscious of the types of relationships you have and aware of the tone you are setting for the relationship with your customers, what they expect of you, and how they perceive you. I am reminded of the CLO who, embarking on a new role in which one of his primary goals was to create a centre of learning expertise, noted a diffidence and lack of confidence in his new staff. He finished his first conversation with the new team by simply reminding them that they were experts and should carry themselves like experts and behave like experts.

Creating a focus on behaviour is a critical foundation in ensuring consistency, which makes it particularly important in corporate learning functions where staff are geographically distributed. Furthermore, it is vital for corporate learning functions to have a *proactive* focus on behaviour because the qualities of people – their behaviour and attitudes – are far more difficult to build and sustain than the qualities of products.[189] The only way to do so is to engage staff in the brand, to help them understand it, own it and want to live it. This is often referred to as internal branding, employee branding or internal marketing,[190] and as a principle it is just as applicable to and important for learning brands as corporate brands. A learning brand thus needs to be more than something that you have; it needs to be something that you do, exhibit and exude. Something that you are!

DEVELOPING A LEARNING BRAND

The six components of a learning brand outlined above are some of the most common and important levers that you can pull to help shape your brand. Many readers, although they may be aware of these issues, may not have actively thought about them in the context of developing a learning brand. Indeed, one of the most common questions I am asked when I present these six components is, 'What practical steps do I need to take to develop a brand and what tips can you give?' With this in mind, let us now consider ten key steps on the way to developing a learning brand.

Be clear on your value

The first step in developing a learning brand is to create a clear strategy that lays out the value you will add to the business and the objectives you will deliver on. It is the promise you make, and all your subsequent activities will be understood and judged in this context. Above all, it needs to be clear about what you will do, how this relates to the broader business strategy, and the difference that it will make to the performance of the organisation and its people. Moreover, having defined your value, you need to make sure that both the business leaders and your function staff understand it, agree with it and fully buy in to it.

Define your customer groups

This step may sound easy and obvious, but in my experience it is often overlooked or skipped as a formal activity. Don't be tempted to do so. In essence you require a 'stakeholder map' to segment your customers and stakeholders into different groups – such as board members, senior executives, high potentials and frontline employees. Be clear about the concerns of each group: what their interest in learning is and what they want from you. It is important not to omit this step because, without a clear understanding of your customer segments, you will not be able to tailor your communications and products to their needs.

Identify how you are currently seen

Do you know how you are viewed now – overall and by each customer group? If not, find out. The best and easiest way is to carry out a quick survey among your customers and stakeholders. Better still would be to carry out annual interviews with them to gather feedback about their perceptions and how they may or may not be changing. Moreover, once you have a picture of your current branding, you need to ask yourself how aligned it is with your strategic objectives, how it might help or hinder achieving these objectives, and also how aligned it is with the wider business's objectives, brand and culture. In other words, can it be improved?

Define your ideal image

Once you are clear on your strategy, customers and current brand, you can start thinking about your ideal brand: the image you would like to convey. A common technique is to identify five or six descriptive words (brand attributes) that describe how you want your function, its work and its people to be viewed. The following tips may be useful. First, focus on the experience that people will have of your function and the value you will contribute to the organisation, rather than on the types of products you deliver. Second, keep it simple; if you can stick to one idea, do so. In other words, try to answer in as few words as possible the old branding question of 'What is the core of your brand?' Ideally, your response should say something about your value to the organisation. Finally, a key consideration has to be your brand's relationship to the organisation and the corporate brand. Will your learning brand seek to use and reinforce the broader business brand at all times, or will you position it not as a separate entity but as an internal partner to the business? Whatever your answers, be clear on what you want to be.

ALIGN BEHIND THE BRAND

Having decided on the brand you wish to build, you need to plan how you will align your function behind it. So, how will your communications, products, materials, places and people communicate this brand and how will observers identify them as part of it? A good place to start is to consider each of the six components outlined above and think about whether and how you will align them.

For example, a simple step that many corporate learning functions already take is to have standardised 'skins' – common colour schemes, fonts and other visual elements that are used in all communications and materials. Some learning functions use logos, which can be effective. But if they are not well executed, they rarely add value; in fact, no logo is better than a poor or confusing one, or indeed too many logos. Likewise, I have seen learning functions invest extraordinary effort in creating straplines – phrases to accompany the logo – yet they are only really beneficial if they are relevant and clever (which often they are not). Thus visual cues can act as powerful signs of the brand that align communications and materials with it, but to be effective they must be simple, consistent and good.

Moreover, it is worth keeping in mind that it may not be possible or desirable to align everything. This is particularly true for functions that are geographically dispersed or operating with a decentralised business model, where ensuring alignment behind the brand can be more challenging. Ownership is a related issue here, in that it will not be possible to brand outsourced open programmes (i.e. ones attended by people from a number of organisations), although outsourced closed programmes can usually be at least jointly branded with the provider. Another issue is that products and materials are much easier to align than services and behaviours. The general rule is that the more coherence there is to your branding, the better it is for the strength and clarity of the brand. The important thing is to be clear about what and how you will align behind the brand.

Test your creations

No marketing director would sign off a new advertising campaign or product launch without test marketing, yet corporate learning functions seem to do this all the time. If you develop new brand visuals, test them out. Try a branded piece with a pilot group. Ask them questions about the brand experience. Take their feedback seriously and adjust things until you get it right.

You could also experiment with a simple technique used by some corporate learning functions – the 'Pepsi Challenge'. You hide the logo and company name on communications and materials such as e-learning documents and then check with pilot groups whether what is left looks as if it could be from any company or is personal to yours. This can be helpful, but remember that familiarity is what is important, not uniqueness: does it feel like you, rather than does it feel different or new?

Create an engagement calendar

Developing a formal engagement plan, often referred to as a marketing plan, is another step that is frequently overlooked. I prefer the term 'engagement' since it conveys more of a sense of 'communicating with' rather than 'communicating to or at'. Of course, the process of engagement should occur at all steps and stages: from obtaining the senior leadership team's buy-in to the learning strategy to involving your team and key stakeholders in defining your ideal brand. I include it here as a separate step, however, because I feel that developing an annual calendar of engagement activities is an additional activity that merits specific mention, since it sets out a clear plan for marketing and communication to each of your different customer and stakeholder segments throughout the year. It is important to remember that what works for one segment may not work for another, but that repetition and consistency in messaging are vital to reinforce the brand.

Marketing/communication channels to consider include your annual learning report, the company's intranet, social media, leadership meetings and the corporate website. If you are creating a new brand image or opening a new facility, launch events can be particularly powerful, as can award ceremonies and special recognition programmes. Finally, in this regard it is essential to consult with your internal communications department – to ensure that you are aligned with other events and communications – and to speak to your marketing department, which can be an excellent resource to help create brand experiences.

Deliver on your promises

Clever names and logos won't mean a thing unless you back them up by delivering on your promises. Indeed, as I have noted, credibility is *the* most important part of the brand image.[191] Moreover, it is critical that you not only deliver on your promises but also prove that you have done so through proper, impact-based evaluation. Confidence in having delivered must come not from belief or hope, but from facts.

Support sustained behaviour

As we all know, it is a lot harder to develop and sustain behaviours than products. So you need to consider whether you have the right competencies to deliver the brand in the desired way, and if not, what you have to do to rectify this. But getting behaviour where you need it to be is just the beginning. You should also have a plan for how to ensure that this behaviour is sustained: that people will continue over time – and often geography – to behave in ways that communicate and reinforce the brand. Here I am talking about the development and support you will offer your staff and how you can keep the brand message alive in employees' minds amid the pressures of everyday organisational life. This is particularly important and challenging when teams are dispersed, or when subject matter experts from outside the learning function assist in developing or delivering programmes. Extra effort is therefore likely to be needed in these scenarios.

Monitor and adapt

The final step in the initial development process is to create a plan for monitoring your brand. This might include activities such as formal evaluations, informal surveys and soliciting feedback from customers and stakeholders. Two things are critical: do not turn this into an industry; and do not stop at collecting this information – act on it and adjust your programmes, communications and behaviours accordingly.

Branding corporate learning

Questions to ask yourself when developing your corporate learning brand

1. What are the promises that your brand currently makes to the business about the role your function will play, the services it will offer, and the impact it will have?
2. How aligned are the strategy, products, looks, names, places and behaviours of your learning function?

---

3. What do the colours, titles and logos used by your learning function communicate?

4. How might business leaders' participation in learning activities be impacted by what your learning currently communicates about the purpose and value of learning?

5. What understanding do learning staff have about the types of behaviour they should exhibit and how this may impact the business' perception of the function?

6. How is the consistent, sustained behaviour of your learning staff supported – especially where they are operating in different locations?

7. Which communication channels will you employ in your engagement plan?

8. What processes do you have in place to monitor the impact of the different elements of your learning brand?

CONCLUDING THOUGHTS

To some, branding always has been and always will be just fluff: about making things look pretty. But it isn't and shouldn't be, especially for a function as image conscious and dependent as corporate learning. In this chapter we have seen that branding corporate learning is not only about *saying* that learning matters, but also about *making* it matter through consistent delivery. And, as current surveys consistently show, many corporate learning functions are desperately in need of a brand makeover. Building and maintaining a strong learning brand need not be expensive, but it takes forethought, focus and consistent performance. The rewards are well worth it; the penalties for doing nothing are severe.

As traditional corporate learning is transformed into an endeavour focused on behaviour change and performance improvement, sustaining these gains has become a key task. It is also one that largely depends on the engagement of learners. More than ever we are being held responsible for learning, yet more than ever we depend upon learners' motivation for our success. If we are passive in facing this challenge, failure is inevitable. We need to employ every with and desire for the learning we offer. Branding is a critical element in the solution; without it our ability to succeed may be significantly limited.

In earlier chapters about the development and delivery of corporate learning, I argued that learning functions need to change what they understand learning to be and to involve: that learning needs to focus on behaviour change and performance improvement, and to be driven by pedagogies rather than technologies. In both this chapter and the previous one on evaluation and reporting, I have tried to convey that learning functions also need to change how their customers and stakeholders see and understand learning. In the next chapter I explore governance and how to keep things on track once these changes have been made.

Case study: creating a learning brand at Nike Inc.

This account of Nike's development of its new corporate learning brand does not specifically follow the models I have presented or speak to all of the issues, but it does provide an insight into a fascinating piece of work to develop a strong and unique corporate learning brand inside one of the most globally recognised corporate brands. Before you read any further, though, I strongly recommend you go to YouTube and look at the NikeU Trailer.* My reaction was: Wow – *that's* an impact brand!

In 2009, Nike Inc. was in the middle of a reorganisation. As part of this, the Global Talent Development (GTD) function was transformed from a highly fragmented and decentralised set of small learning teams to a global function providing a wide range of solutions. The mandate of this new function was simple and clear: to provide Nike employees with the leadership, management and functional skills they needed to succeed in their roles.

To head up this new function, Nike hired Andrew Kilshaw as chief learning officer. For the first three months, he undertook a

---

* www.youtube.com/watch?v=NOtzCPJ8-tA&feature=youtu.be.

systematic diagnosis of how GTD was working, asking for suggestions and advice from the 70 employees he oversaw and from key
stakeholders and customers. Through these early conversations
he built up a clear picture of what was going on and a core of committed supporters. 'It was inquiry instead of advocacy', he said. 'I
learned *and* got their buy-in at the same time.'

Kilshaw identified two challenges that he realised were key in
ensuring that the function was successful in delivering value. First, he
would need to develop an operational model that was driven by a central agenda yet also catered to the highly individualised needs of business units and geographies. It was a thin line to walk: too central a
model and local needs would not be met; too local and there would be
a lack of coherence and common strategy. Kilshaw also realised that
finding the right operating model would not be enough: the second
challenge he faced was to help his team to walk this same thin line
between central and local and to think as one function, while operating as a dispersed group. And one of the first things that Kilshaw had
noticed about his new team was that although Nike operated in many
countries, they had not yet adopted a global mindset. 'People didn't
really understand their roles as part of a global team', he explained.
'They functioned separately rather than in a matrix.'

The answer to both these challenges, Kilshaw knew, lay in developing something that bound the function and its activities together
while enabling local activity, something that allowed his team to
'think globally, while acting locally'. What he needed was not just a
new operating model but a compelling brand to glue it all together.

'During my first three months at Nike, I asked around: "What do
you think of Global Talent Development?" The answer was often
ambiguous, with some thinking we ran recruiting. It was clear that
although we'd reorganised the people in the function, our internal
consumer base did not know this. We had a huge opportunity to create a brand and a name for ourselves across the 38,000 and growing
employees within Nike.'

Kilshaw presented his vision and a detailed plan to the HR executive team and, with their support and blessing, took his story on the

road to the global HR business partner community as well as key business stakeholders. Yet with the opportunity clear and buy-in achieved, some big questions still needed answering, most notably: 'For one of the most iconic brand companies in the world, what exactly could and should a learning brand look like?'

To guide their work, Kilshaw and his team identified five components of their ideal brand – what they wanted their consumers to say about the function aspirationally. These were defined as follows:

1. We are easy to access.
2. We are easy to do business with.
3. We are catalysts for learning, not just providers of learning.
4. We provide access to the right learning, at the right time in the right way.
5. Our heritage and history are our orange thread.

Realising that they needed specialist expertise, they enlisted internal marketing support and an external brand agency to help define the mood (the feelings that the brand should evoke), the function's name and language, and the visual look and feel. They thought that like Nike's consumers, the learning brand should feel connected to sport, dynamic and unconventional. In terms of the name, they played on the existence of a few internal universities, such as Merchandising University and Lean Business Solutions University, to create an umbrella brand called NikeU. However, the team decided that U should not stand for university alone; they created a more multidimensional and culturally acceptable message with U standing for *you, us, unleashing potential, unconventional learning, unlimited capability.*

Purposefully, the brand was designed to reflect Nike Inc., rather than being a sub-brand of the HR function: to support the brand truth that NikeU is a catalyst for learning (connecting learners directly with one another within functions), and to ensure that all employees – not just HR – know they are accountable for actively driving the learning community at Nike.

Next came the visual brand and a go-to-market architecture (how the function would organise and name its offerings). In a play on the company's sporting roots, each offering was described as a 'track', for example The Leader Track, The Manager Track and The Pro Track, with tools and resources being packaged in The Coach's Gym Bag. A cross-functional community of practice was then assembled to explore how the brand experience, as well as the visual brand, should be built into people's roles, operational processes, communications and learning experiences. Kilshaw hoped to emulate branding experts such as Virgin Atlantic, for which every touchpoint reinforces the uniqueness of its service compared with more 'vanilla' competitors. It was not just about a new logo or template. The learning community hard launched the brand across all of Nike Inc. in 2012 with the introduction of the NikeU intranet site.

So Kilshaw identified what his function needed to do to add value to the business. He engaged the support of his team, stakeholders and the broader business in developing the solution, identified how his function was currently seen, and thought about the ideal image he wanted to create. Then he aligned the function and its activities behind this brand, before finally engaging the broader business in it and starting on the process of delivering it. Building a brand is hard work, but it's amazing what one can do, and for the GTD function it was strategically critical, providing a binding force that allowed it to be far more flexible, localised and varied in its offerings. And the video? I am not sure if it would have value in every business, but it is hard to dispute that it really does have the 'wow' factor.

8   Governing corporate learning: ensuring oversight and accountability

We have looked at how to develop a clear, mandated strategy; at how and who you need to successfully operationalise this strategy; and at how to evaluate and then communicate its value. How, though, do you hold this all together and sustain it over time? The answer is *governance*. As words go, it may not sound that thrilling, but it is as inevitable as it is important and therefore deserves attention.

Sooner or later, at some point along the path to maturity, learning functions face the need for governance. To be clear here, I am not talking about normal decision-making channels, but a decision-making body that oversees the activity of the learning function and that is separate or independent from hierarchical reporting lines. In some businesses good learning governance may be achieved through the normal channels, but in most, contained as they are within the existing company structure, these channels are not sufficient for performing a business-wide oversight role. So something extra is required.

It often begins with a business simply trying to get to grips with inefficiencies in spending, perhaps after discovering, for example, that it has multiple LMSs in use or duplicate learning programmes in different parts of the organisation. Other times, it may be driven by a desire to create a more strategic and enterprise-wide approach to capability development. Frequently, it happens without there even being a designated CLO or a recognisable central learning function.

However you get there, governance is about bringing things together. It is about how organisations get learning done systematically and with the whole business in mind.[192] It is about how they ensure the strategic alignment of learning activities with business objectives and the effective balancing of local and enterprise-wide learning needs. And it is about the structures, processes and practices that enable all this to happen and thereby make learning work better for the entire organisation.

THE BENEFITS OF GOOD GOVERNANCE

There is plenty of research pointing out the benefits of good learning governance. At a broad level, research has shown that there is a very strong relationship between having learning governance structures in place, such as steering groups, and the perceived efficacy of the learning function.[193] In other words, learning functions that are seen as effective do good governance. As for how exactly governance helps improve functions' performance, there is no single and simple link, but research and experience suggest eight contributions that effective governance can make:

1. *Efficiency.* Probably the most visible benefit and the most achievable in short timescales, this includes creating economies of scale with vendors, streamlining learning programmes to eliminate those that are duplicates or redundant, and ensuring that the learning function is suitably and adequately resourced to deliver on its objectives. It is often the biggest driver for governance structures to be established, or at least the most cited rationale for it – and little wonder, since the size of inefficiencies in large corporations can extend into millions of dollars.

2. *Alignment.* The use of steering groups to ensure that learning activities are aligned with business objectives at both a business unit and an enterprise-wide level is probably the second most commonly cited benefit of governance. A related benefit is that steering groups can help ensure that learning activities in different parts of a business are aligned, thereby preventing different programmes from undermining one another or being too diffuse in their objectives. In this vein, good governance has also been shown to be useful in avoiding and resolving turf wars and conflicts that might otherwise fester.

3. *Ownership.* Using a board-like structure as a governance body helps involve the wider organisation in the business of learning, spreading the sense of accountability beyond the learning function and HR,

thereby creating a shared sense of ownership of learning across the business. Given the research showing how critical the work environment is in supporting behaviour change, having this shared sense of ownership can be vital in delivering real and sustained performance improvement.

4. *Accountability*. Research has also shown that there is a strong correlation between the existence of a governance steering group and the likelihood that an organisation will have an established measurement and evaluation programme.[194] Governance can create greater accountability just by creating a focus on investment and value. A less recognised fact is that governance can also promote accountability by enabling better metrics, i.e. the more consistent processes and infrastructures that generally come with governance can improve access to standardised data and thereby enhance analysis and reporting of the business impact of learning investments.

5. *Quality*. Simply put, governance can improve the quality of learning initiatives across the business by setting minimum standards, enabling the sharing of best practices, and creating visibility on outcomes.

6. *Coordination*. With the emergence and growth of enterprise-wide learning initiatives, corporate learning functions are increasingly finding culture change and change management on their agendas. With such initiatives, progress and success can be hard to achieve unless the many business units and teams concerned are involved in supporting the development, delivery and management of these programmes. Thus, having a structure that brings these stakeholders together can significantly facilitate the process of involving and coordinating them.

7. *Communication*. Governance groups can increase the visibility of the learning function's work and ease access to communication channels into business units. They can also aid communication back into the learning function, enhancing its ability to identify learning needs.
   An automotive financial services company I worked with provides an interesting example of how the governance body of a corporate academy contributed to the business through foresight and open communication.
   Like many captive organisations operating in a challenging global market, this organisation saw its margins shrinking and repeated cyclical declines in its traditional business. A member of the governance group

foresaw that the business would start developing fleet management solutions to generate counter-cyclical sources of revenue and communicated this to the corporate academy. To compensate for the shortage of fleet management experts in the market, the academy developed a portfolio of offerings to prepare some employees to transition to this business so that, when the time came, they were ready. Two years on, the company has completed two fleet management acquisitions, significantly aided by the individuals it had the foresight to train to grow this business.

8. *Resourcing*. Last, but by no means least, in businesses without a central budget for learning activities, a governance group can provide easier access to the required capital[195] and resources. For example, in a decentralised business I recently worked with, the central learning function identified an enterprise-wide learning need to improve performance management. Through the governance group, it secured agreement from each business unit leader to help fund the development of the programme, the cost associated with attendance, and the resourcing of temporary headcount to oversee the administration of the programme.

THE CHALLENGE OF GOOD GOVERNANCE

This long list of benefits raises the question of why it seems to be so difficult for many corporate learning functions to achieve an effective governance body. One of the most common reasons I find is lack of interest from the broader business and an unwillingness to get involved. With the exception of a few CEOs and top executives who are truly committed to the future capability of the organisation, many top executives do not see learning governance as part of their role. In fact, the most recent CIPD study, published in 2010, indicates that although executives generally view learning and talent management as key priorities for their companies, only 20 per cent of them have ongoing structured discussions on these issues and only 10 per cent do so at board level.

Interestingly, I have also encountered the opposite of this challenge – a level of support that is too robust. This can occur when a corporate learning function is strongly connected to the CEO and may even have been his or her brainchild. Often there is the assumption that because such functions are so well positioned they do not have to worry about governance. However, time and again I have seen them disconnected from the business, perceived as the CEO's toy, out of touch and separate from the real action. In some cases, they may also be disconnected from a resentful HR department, which continues to carry out core HR processes such as performance management, succession planning and talent pool development without consulting them. In fact, this was precisely the scenario I found at a global bank I worked with: the corporate business school was established by the CEO and reported directly to him for a number of years until it was decided that its agenda would be better served if it reported to HR. With this change and the arrival of a new learning leader, a more holistic governance structure was put in place, and recent reports indicate a higher level of support across the organisation and a better integration of key offerings.

Politics and money inevitably add to the governance challenges. At a multinational oil and gas company I worked with, the learning governance body identified a key need for the refining side of the business to boost its learning offering. However, because of the high profitability of the smaller exploration business and the strong positions of its heads on the company's board, most company-wide learning initiatives tended to be driven by exploration's needs and exploration tended to get the lion's share of the company-wide learning budget, even though it had many fewer people working for it than the refining side. The governance body was unable to change the situation because of the politics and, as a result, performance problems continued across the refining sites.

A related, fundamental challenge is that of control. A rationale of governance and alignment for the 'greater good' is almost always accompanied by anxiety at local levels. Business units worry that control from the top will spoil the local characteristics that make their programmes effective, and on occasion I have seen these fears fuelled by heavy-handed and ill-judged efforts by senior management to bring learning under control.

IMPLEMENTING GOVERNANCE

Although organisations trying to implement effective governance face a number of hurdles, they do appear to be moving towards greater governance. A recent study showed that 59 per cent of the organisations surveyed had some type of steering committee in place, a significant increase on the number of such structures found at the turn of the millennium.[196] Driving this new focus on governance are two issues that have historically been challenges, namely money and control. The recent downturn has in fact been a stimulus for governance, since tighter budgets have resulted in a sharper focus on how effectively money is being spent, and consequently greater need for control. Yet the trend seems to be continuing beyond the downturn, with some researchers citing corporate learning functions' increasingly large investments in technology as the single biggest driver of governance structures. Simply put, the organisations making these significant investments tend to want to have some sort of oversight in place. In support of this hypothesis, according to the study cited above, 82 per cent of the organisations with a steering committee had some representation from IT in these groups.

So whether we are talking about governance of a central learning function, governance of a specific learning project, or even governance of company-wide learning activities, it appears to be a growing, if overdue, trend. The stimuli seem to involve either shared budgets or shared use of a learning resource (such as an LMS), which brings together people from across a business unit or even the whole enterprise. The first step tends to be the formation of a steering committee or learning council, and once such a decision-making body has been created, it usually puts in place the processes, tools and infrastructure required to manage and track the results of its decisions.

For many organisations, this is as far as they have gone. Yet for me, as welcome as these measures are, one of the critical steps required for truly effective governance is still missing, namely a common planning process. In the survey described above, although 59 per cent of organisations reported having some type of steering

committee, more than 80 per cent of the surveyed businesses did not
have an enterprise-wide plan for learning.

Without a central plan, learning activities remain fragmented
across business units or geographies and there is no place to consider
and uniformly act upon enterprise-wide capability needs. For a governance body to be truly effective, it has to go beyond simple oversight of spending or arbitration to resolve the conflicting demands
of key stakeholders. Through joint planning, it can create a process
for bringing together different views, ensure that a strategic debate
about direction and priorities takes place, and see that the organisation profits from a united and holistic portfolio of offerings. When
it comes to behaviour and culture change, for the business to move
forward as a whole, everyone must move in the same direction.

A lack of central planning and the consequent lack of central
reporting is why most organisations I have worked with and surveyed still feel they have a long way to go before they can tick the
governance box on their strategic plan. So how do you go about it?

Whether you are beginning to devise a learning governance
system or seeking to improve what you currently have, you first
need to be clear about what you are trying to accomplish, and why,
and to determine your organisation's readiness for the change. The
less ready it is, the more convincing and corralling it will require.
The first logistical step for most is to determine the membership
of the board-like structure that will carry out governance, be it a
local learning committee or a central steering group. And it is a
critical step, too, because the decision about who sits on the governance body will play a key role in determining the long-term success and, in some cases, even the survival of the corporate learning
function.

CREATING THE GOVERNANCE GROUP

What sort of people do you require? First and foremost, it is important to choose members who have both the right status and the right
attitude. They should have corporate clout and true commitment to
driving the corporate learning agenda. Importantly, members should

be formally or informally approved by the CEO to ensure that any recommendations are taken seriously.

In most organisations these criteria alone will generate a pretty short shortlist, yet members should not be restricted to the 'usual suspects'. They need to be appointed from across the business unit or organisation, and not be just those who are typically involved in learning. A common mistake I have witnessed in a number of organisations is that membership of the governance body is drawn only from HR people from different parts of the business. Although these players are important and are essential partners at the operational level, they should not be the dominant power on the governance body. Ideally HR should be represented by one person – preferably the head of corporate HR – and all other members should represent a cross-section of the business. This helps to establish clearly that learning and development are management responsibilities and not relegated to a support function.

In addition to the internal players, it can be useful to invite an external expert or two to join the governance group. This can help forestall any self-interest on the part of insiders, ensure that more objective input is provided in case of disagreements, and introduce cutting-edge practice in the areas of leadership development, management and/or professional excellence into the curriculum. External experts can be drawn from a number of different fields. In the case of a multinational pharmaceutical business I have studied, the governance body included a business school professor with expertise in corporate strategy and clear specialisation in the industry; he provided ongoing external input, alongside that provided by the business executives. In another case, a senior partner of a reputable consulting firm played such a role. And in the case of a global utility business, there was 'rotating responsibility', with different external partners being brought in at different times to provide input and ensure honest discussions were taking place among the governance board members based on new points of focus in the business's strategy.

In terms of numbers, although all critical stakeholders should be represented, it is also important to ensure that the group does not become too large. Studies looking at executive boards have discovered a negative relationship between board size and performance[197] – in other words, the bigger your board, the less well your company is likely to perform. This is because there are likely to be more conflicts of interest in decision-making, and larger boards allow members to be more passive in their membership.[198] The recommended size for a governance group is not fixed, but I suggest a maximum of eight to ten for an organisation-wide group, and five to six for a business unit level group.

As for tenure, I recommend that it should be time limited and, ideally, should not exceed two or three years, to allow for ongoing renewal of the governance body and to continually feed the developmental agenda with new ideas and perspectives. Changes in membership mean that, over time, different parts of the organisation are seeded with people who are more developmentally oriented and are better able to link development to their daily operations.

Of course, attracting the right people is not always as straightforward as identifying them. In some organisations, there is a degree of kudos in being part of the governance group: the CEO sends personal letters inviting key executives to join and thanks them for their contribution at year-end or when their tenure is up. Other organisations go even further and include the nomination of governance members in the proceedings of board meetings. I have found that, in most cases, CLOs who take the time to build a clear positioning of the strategic role of governance group membership are able to attract the right members for this task. These executives take their jobs seriously, and it is obvious from interviews I have had with them that they take pride in contributing to the development of individuals and the organisation as part of their legacy.

THE ROLE OF THE GOVERNANCE GROUP

Whatever shape the governance body takes, to be truly effective its *raison d'être* needs to be more than merely monitoring spend and the progress of projects. It should be designed to be a strategic partner of the corporate learning function, charged with ensuring that the whole learning portfolio is more than the sum of its parts, that different sections of the organisation are not reinventing the wheel, and that the learning function serves as an incubator of new ideas and innovation. Yet more than a few corporate learning functions I have observed have put together governance boards with highly reputable members representing key parts of the business, but have failed to harvest any of the benefits. Usually this happens because the roles of this body have not been well defined, so the management team has not known how best to leverage it.

Clearly, the roles and responsibilities of governing bodies will and should vary between organisations. As key areas for consideration, though, I suggest six potential roles and associated responsibilities. With each, a critical decision will be whether the governance group will own and be accountable for the task (e.g. strategy or risk management), or whether they will simply advise on the issue while the CLO retains accountability. I suggest that, in principle, ownership is what the group should aspire to, though I am aware that in many if not most businesses this will not be an immediate practical or political possibility. What is important is that for each of the six roles, ownership and accountability are clearly defined and agreed. Written up as a job description, the six roles are:

Strategy

Following the idea that strategy is about the development of intentional, informed and integrated choices,[199] one of the key roles of any learning governance group is to advise and provide input to both this choice-making process and the subsequent decision-making. The group needs to:

- Provide ongoing strategic input into the state of the organisation and its industry, as well as individual business units.
- Ensure alignment between different stakeholder groups on the operating principles, goals and scope of the learning function.
- Ensure alignment between the scope of the learning function, the portfolio of offerings and the design of the learning organisation.
- Participate in the selection and support of the CLO.

Planning

A second role is planning how the learning strategy will be implemented and to:

- Develop an annual learning plan for the business.
- Anticipate future needs and ensure that the corporate learning function is proactive in setting the future learning agenda.
- Act as a decision-making body accountable for making choices about learning priorities.
- Ensure the overall portfolio is coherent and addresses the needs of the business.

Financial stewardship

Related to the planning process is the issue of budgetary regulation. Here the governance group's role is to:

- Ensure the corporate learning function is financially accountable, by reviewing both spending and the return on it.
- Approve and review budgets and their allocation based on business requirements, making sure that investments are linked to and support the realisation of organisational strategy.
- Provide additional funds and resources where appropriate (e.g. where little or no central learning budget exists).

Operational support

Although this is sometimes overlooked, the governance group's potential to provide critical support for the implementation of learning initiatives is very significant. It can:

- Provide communication channels to various lines of the business, cascading the vision, mission and key priorities of the corporate learning function.
- Serve as the voice of the customer, collecting critical input on performance gaps and competency building priorities of the various business units or functions.
- Champion learning by promoting learning programmes and products and demonstrating executive commitment to learning as a strategic enabler.

- Ensure that the environment required for successful learning initiatives is present within business areas (e.g. level of managerial support and cultural issues).

Risk management

The task most commonly associated with the word 'governance' is probably risk management – and for good reason. And this is one of the key roles of learning governance groups, which:

- Provide checks and balances to the operational day-to-day management of the learning function.
- Ensure that the corporate learning function has identified potential risks to the successful delivery of the annual learning plan.
- Make sure that risk management and contingency plans are in place where appropriate.

Monitoring

The role of monitoring the implementation of the learning strategy and annual learning plan is critical, because governance can only maximise the efficacy and efficiency of learning activities if an effective feedback loop is in place. Or, to put it another way, you can't adjust your aim if you don't know you're missing. Governance groups need to:

- Oversee how initiatives are tied to business metrics and thus how learning impact is measured.
- Review learning initiative evaluations and ensure that conclusions are acted on to drive continuous improvement.
- Provide regular reports to the executive management team, including an annual learning report.

MAKING THE GOVERNANCE GROUP WORK

So you've brought people to the table and clarified their roles, but how do you get them to work well together? The dynamics of any group obviously depend on its make-up, and in this respect some groups immediately gel while others require support to get them working effectively together. Never take effective dynamics for granted!

The first step is to create clarity on attendance. Ideally, the governance group should come together quarterly to discuss strategic and operational issues. In practice, however, what seems to work in most cases is a minimum of two meetings a year. One such meeting should take place in the fourth quarter in order to agree on key priorities and finalise an overall learning plan for the following year. The second meeting should take place in the second quarter to assess the overall state of delivery and impact, evaluate progress and make the proper adjustments and mid-course corrections to the portfolio and delivery channels, based on feedback and any emerging new demands.

Moving beyond such simple logistics, let us now consider the all-important question of information. Describing how highly effective executive boards function, Ram Charan cited *information architecture* as one of the three critical building blocks that make boards so strong.[200] It refers to how boards get information, what information they get, and what form it is in. Charan observed that when there is too much or too little data or when it is poorly presented, boards spend too much of their meeting time questioning the meaning of the data they have received and not enough time attending to their core tasks and the consequences of this data. The effective functioning of governance groups thus depends on the quality, the timeliness and the format of the information they receive. In my experience, this is unfortunately not given sufficient attention.

Next, to function effectively the group needs to be more than just a bureaucratic body that signs off on proposals: it has to question, contend and debate. In this vein, it is a good idea to use an external professional facilitator for the first few meetings, to encourage open debate and support closure and consensus building. The facilitator should also have one-on-one meetings with members to ensure that concerns that are not shared at the meetings are subsequently aired. Other popular ways to promote open relationships and healthy debate include encouraging informal exchanges between members over a shared meal and celebrating key milestones in the learning function together.

Finally, to sum up, I believe there are three critical characteristics that highly effective governance groups should aspire to have:

the members should know what they need to know to make good decisions; they should be committed to saying what has to be said so good decisions can be made; and they should monitor their own effectiveness. Although this last point is often overlooked, the governance group needs to commit to evaluating itself as a group and individually, in terms of their contribution and the value they add. This brings us back to our starting point: that learning governance exists to make learning work better for the entire organisation. As with any objective, key performance indicators are essential, including an evaluation of whether they have been met.

Governing corporate learning

Questions to ask to help ensure oversight and accountability

1. Is there a central governance group in place, primarily consisting of business leaders of the right status and with the right attitude, representing all critical stakeholders?
2. Is the role of the governance group clearly defined and agreed upon by all key stakeholders? Does it function as a strategic advisor to the learning functions as well as providing oversight of activity and spend?
3. How good is attendance at the governance group?
4. How does the governance group receive information? Is it of good quality, relevant, timely and in an appropriate format? Is there a process in place to check this?
5. Is there an agreed central learning plan in place? Is there a regular reporting process for reviewing progress against the plan?
6. How does the governance group currently provide support for the implementation of learning initiatives?
7. Does the governance group function effectively at present as a voice of the customer?
8. What are the key performance indicators of the governance group? What is the process for reviewing progress against these?

CONCLUDING THOUGHTS

If evaluation is how we sharpen our steel and ensure that what we do works, governance is how we keep it sharp so that it continues to work. So, as boring as the word may sound, governance is a critical piece of the learning puzzle. Indeed, I would go so far as to say that without good governance, without such a mechanism to check and adjust what we are doing, it is inevitable that the functional alignment of learning activities will deteriorate over time. You can get your strategy right, resource your function with experts, design innovative interventions, demonstrate unequivocally the value of what you do, and develop a brilliant brand. But it is not enough. Because if you want to sustain it all, you need good governance.

Case study: creating good governance at Novartis

Global companies can be exceedingly complex, with multiple cultures internally, operating within and across further multiple cultures externally. Typically, each division or business unit has its own specific culture and it operates across different countries, each with its own set of societal norms. Thus it is hardly surprising that one-size-fits-all solutions to corporate learning rarely work in big global organisations.

At a very basic level, employee learning needs are likely to differ between countries. In these scenarios, the best structural option for learning is a hybrid blend of decentralised learning teams in combination with a strong central corporate function. Making a hybrid model work, however, can be far from easy. It is not as simple as just establishing a corporate university with training departments all over the world. To hold these different units together, manage the inevitable tensions and deal with logistical issues such as duplicated programmes, standardising reporting and setting minimum standards demands that little extra. It demands governance.

In 2010, Novartis decided to build a bridge between the central corporate learning team and the various decentralised learning teams dotted around the world. This bridge – *the Learning Board* – was a governing body. Mandated with full support from senior executives, the board was thus designed to be a decision-making body that determined – by majority vote – the strategy and operations of both the central corporate learning function and its decentralised counterparts. The specific objectives of the board were:

- To define a company-wide, integrated learning strategy that was aligned with both company and HR strategies, and to coordinate and supervise the implementation of the strategy throughout the company.
- To determine the learning budget and allocate resources for learning teams to function effectively.
- To define the tools and processes required to implement the strategy and maximise the impact of spending.
- To make cross-divisional decisions on learning policy for review and endorsement by the HR board, and to be in charge of implementing the HR board's decisions throughout the company (the Learning Board is accountable to the HR board).
- To focus on company-wide people manager and generic skills training.

The board consisted of thirteen senior level representatives from all divisions and regions. Each business division represented had one casting vote, irrespective of the number of board members present. When conflicts arose – as they inevitably do – the chairman was charged with balancing opinions. The individuals chosen as members recognised the overall value of learning for the company and knew how to keep their egos in check. They were appointed by each division's business leader and were selected from talent management, HR and learning roles.

The benefits of introducing the Learning Board were considerable. By sharing knowledge and achieving economies of scale, learning costs were lowered and standards and quality rose. The largest cost savings came from avoiding programme overlap, and the biggest gain in quality came through sharing expertise and agreement over consistent standards. In addition, agreement on standard metrics enabled the Learning Board to gain a broader and more sophisticated understanding of the impact of their learning investments.

So the Learning Board brought people together, created a forum for discussion and tension resolution, and enabled the various learning teams to operate in a functionally aligned manner. For Novartis, the governance provided by the Learning Board has enabled a potentially complex hybrid structure to function effectively.

9 A way forward: creating a context for learning

I began this book with a crisis, some worry and some concern. The catharsis of writing has unfortunately done little to assuage this anxiety; indeed seeing it all in black and white has probably only served to heighten my feelings. My concerns were two-fold: the lack of progress in improving the standing of corporate learning, despite significant amounts of effort and activity; and a horrible suspicion that some in the learning field may feel that the difficulties we face are just skin-deep, matters of presentation and positioning.

In the preceding chapters I have made the case against this skin-deep theory of the crisis in corporate learning. I have shown how the stark and painful reality is that from top to toe something is not right. When nearly half of learning functions do not have a clear and mandated mission; when the development of learning solutions is weighed down by traditional academic approaches on the one hand and dazzled by the shiny promises of new technologies on the other; and when only 10 to 15 per cent of learning functions are monitoring the impact of what they do, how could it be otherwise?

Some people may think that this is overly harsh and at odds with what has been written elsewhere. After all, the journals are brimming with wonderful case studies of things done well and going right. I have mixed feelings about this press. It feels great to read these inspirational stories of how different people in different places have found innovative ways to make learning work. And yet, taken as a whole, as a body of literature, the radiantly positive tone of it all feels far removed from the reality of the persistently poor satisfaction ratings that corporate learning receives from business leaders. Indeed it is these poor ratings – with satisfaction levels hovering around 20 per cent, remember – that show the sheer size of the task ahead. Merely doubling or trebling them will not be sufficient. We need to quadruple them, improve them by a staggering 400 per cent, before we can start saying that corporate learning is in a good place. So I do sometimes wonder if all this positive coverage is inadvertently masking the difficulties we face and undermining the sense of urgency that I feel is required to turn things around.

In light of this, it may seem surprising that I also began this book with hope, noting that although we may be under greater pressure to deliver than ever before, this also means that we have the stage and thus the opportunity to put things right. Business leaders still seem to believe in the link between learning spend and business performance. As a profession, we do some really good work. And for all the stereotypes about people in the field, some of which are unfortunately based in fact, the learning profession does have some excellent people and a rich seam of expertise to mine. So there *is* hope and, for all my dire warnings, worries and concerns, it is with hope that I finish this book.

Some of this hope stems from the fact that corporate learning functions are increasingly reporting a shift in focus from individual learning to organisational learning – from improving individual abilities to improving the capabilities of the business as a whole. In fact, nearly 60 per cent of respondents to a recent McKinsey survey reported that building organisational capabilities was a top priority for them. This shift may seem subtle, but it is a critical one, since it makes corporate learning directly responsible for ensuring that organisations are able to do what they need to do in order to deliver good results. It thus provides learning functions with a rationale and an opportunity to be agenda setters.

Clothing retailer Gap Inc. is an example of a company that has found a way to use learning to do more than just learning. Like a few other companies, it has adapted internal leadership programmes, initially designed for Gap's executives, to use with leaders from external partner organisations. The particularly innovative aspect of Gap's work is that it provides the programmes free of charge to its

North American non-profit partners, to help them learn new strategy frameworks, hone their talent development skills, and develop their abilities to leverage peers as thought partners. The programme thus leverages Gap's learning expertise to help its partners maximise their community impact. In doing so, it is putting the learning function at the centre of Gap's relationship with the broader community and its work in corporate social responsibility.

WHAT WE NEED TO DO

Throughout this book I have not described or advocated a *single big idea* because I do not think that one thing alone will be enough to create the shift required. Instead, I have presented lots of smaller, interrelated ideas.

I suggested at the beginning that the aim in doing so was to try to create a tipping point that would launch corporate learning on a new, upward trajectory. Yet I know that piling up a whole host of changes will not necessarily trigger a tipping point to disrupt the status quo. I am aware, too, that one of the risks of presenting so many smaller suggestions is that it can be hard to see the wood for the trees, to see what is truly important. So I thought that I would finish my story that began with a crisis with a brief summary of what I believe are the most important changes that need to happen in order to end the crisis. Five key priorities stand out.

Focus on functionalism

The first priority should come as no surprise, given my emphasis in previous chapters on functionalism: on ensuring that what you do is aligned with what you need to do and with what the business needs from you. And I am advocating a continuing, unrelenting focus on functionalism, not a half-hearted approach. In my eyes, adopting a functionalist approach is a little like being pregnant: it is something you either are or are not.

Much of the thinking about learning during the past decade has been about how learning functions need to be strategically aligned with external elements, with the company's business objectives and its prevailing culture and ways of doing things. This is undoubtedly an important aspect of functionalism, too, and is critical to the success of learning functions. In order to translate this strategic alignment into operational results, however, learning functions also need to focus on how their internal components, processes and people are functionally aligned with one another. External strategic alignment, then, is only half the picture; it is of little use unless it is accompanied by internal functional alignment.

I have also tried to show that it is not always easy to know whether your learning function and its objectives, components and activities are functionally aligned. The path to functionalism is littered not only with big and obvious challenges like aligning objectives with business strategy but also with subtle ones, concealed in some of our most basic assumptions about what learning is and involves. This leads to the second priority.

Focus on corporate learning, not academic learning

We, as corporate learning professionals, need to shrug off the shackles of the traditions and assumptions of academic learning. This may be easier said than done, tied as they are to our own experiences of what learning is. Yet it is important that we do free ourselves from them because corporate learning *is* fundamentally different from academic learning. To use a stereotype: academic learning is primarily focused on inputs, what is taught and what is learned or taken in, while corporate learning is primarily interested in outputs, how the things we learn are used, and how they can be of value to individuals and organisations.

This does not mean that there is no place for traditional academic learning in organisations, especially when it comes to technical training or the development of innovative new ideas or products. But there does need to be a fundamental shift to recognise that, in the majority of organisations, most learning occurs within the framework, traditions and expectations of corporate learning rather than of academic learning.

In a practical sense, the single biggest part of this shift will involve a move from talking about learning to talking about sustained behaviour change. In this regard, and as noted in Chapter 4, the rising application of the principles of *gameification* will be critical, as will the incorporation of research and ideas from other fields involved in behaviour change, such as behavioural economics and psychotherapy. For those immediately cautious about the term 'psychotherapy', let's be clear: I am not advocating putting our leaders 'on the couch'. Rather, I am simply suggesting that we should be proactive and willing to look to other fields for ideas on how to succeed in what is essentially an extremely difficult task, and indeed one that is far more challenging than merely communicating new knowledge or skills.

Step in and out of the business

The late psychologist Bruno Bettleheim once allegedly said that the challenge in changing another's behaviour is not so much being able to step inside the client's head, to understand her motivations and thinking, as being able to step out again in order to think objectively about what needs to happen. To my mind, this is the very issue now facing corporate learning. With all the focus on aligning with business needs, demonstrating value to the business, and developing organisational capabilities, there is the risk that we might step in too far and lose our ability to be objective about what needs to happen. And if we are to achieve and retain credibility as agenda setters, we need to be able to contribute an alternative viewpoint to what already exists.

Part of the challenge here is a legacy issue, common to many of the HR and learning functions I have seen: namely, self-consciousness about how they are commonly viewed and a strong desire to be seen in a positive light. There is nothing unusual about wanting to be perceived positively, of course, but it becomes a potentially negative issue when it is a key driver rather than merely a consideration, since it can constrain the ability to act. The recent research showing that learning leaders' primary concern is demonstrating their worth to the business may well reflect current budgetary constraints and learning's generally poor standing in business leaders' eyes, but it may also reflect some of this self-consciousness and is thus a cause for concern.

Whatever the underlying issues, if learning functions are to add value they have to find a way to balance the need to be an integral part of the business with an equally strong ability to step outside it, take an objective view and apply, without bias, their expertise in pedagogy and learning science to the task at hand.

Apply market forces

As I noted in Chapter 6, corporate learning is effectively a market with competing products and services, and if we as professionals want quality, efficacy and efficiency to prevail, we need to apply market forces. By this I mean that we need to be able to compare products and know what works and what doesn't, so that we can make informed judgements about what we want to do, what we can do and what we need to do. And to do this, we need to get evaluation and reporting right.

And herein lies the problem: for all the talk and ideas over the past forty years we have by and large failed to improve the quality of learning evaluation. Faulty and incomplete models, limited resources and lack of expertise have all been cited as culprits. And there is little doubt that each of these has played its part. Yet after forty years of inertia, I cannot help but wonder if there is a lack of will in play, too – a general lack of desire to evaluate. After all, almost everyone has something to lose from rigorous evaluation, and it is in very few stakeholders' interests to find out – or, even worse, admit – that a learning programme has not been successful. And I cannot believe that this dynamic has not affected learning functions' eagerness to undertake impact evaluation.

Of course, it is not only learning functions that are at fault here: one can hardly blame their reluctance, occurring as it does in the current context of failure not being tolerated or at least not forgotten. So any improvement in current evaluation practice is unlikely to happen until businesses understand that learning is a complex and difficult systemic task that is not only the result of the learning function's efforts. This message may not be easy to hear, but it needs to be heard, because without proper evaluation we cannot apply market forces, and without this we cannot make informed decisions. And without that, corporate learning risks descending into mediocrity (or indeed, depending upon your viewpoint, remaining there).

Bring the business to bear and to account

In Chapter 1, I told the tale of the Big Idea that was the *learning organisation* and how, despite all the promise and potential, it eventually faltered. The idea it promoted was to create an organisational culture that supported learning; that enabled it, encouraged it and rewarded it; that made it an integral part of what we do, day in day out. It was a laudable ideal, but it ultimately failed because its concepts could not easily be translated into operational processes and practices, and because it was difficult to link its objectives to organisations' commercial priorities.

Yet we should not take this failure to mean it was a bad idea. For all its faults and foibles, one of the many things that the learning organisation movement got absolutely right was the importance of the culture and context in which learning occurs. As I described in Chapter 3 on developing learning solutions, subsequent research has been clear on the matter, showing that contextual factors such as the workplace environment are actually *more* important in ensuring the application of learning than the quality of the learning event. This is pretty staggering when you think about it.

It is high time that learning functions make this link loud and clear. If they don't, no one else will. As noted earlier, according to a recent survey, 71 per cent of respondents stated that their organisation expects managerial support as part of the learning process. However, when asked what managers are expected to do, 63 per cent stated that they are only required to formally endorse the programme, and only 23 per cent reported that managers have to physically do something, such as hold pre- and post-training discussions. Saying 'I support you' while doing nothing to back it up is not support, and learning functions need to make this clear.

This will undoubtedly be a politically fraught task in many organisations, but if learning functions are to succeed, they need to find a way of bringing organisations to account and thereby play their part. I believe the only way to achieve this is to have a solidly mandated mission; to use learning proposals to clarify what all parties must do to change behaviour and keep it changed; and to use proper impact evaluation to assess each party's contribution. Learning functions must not and simply cannot accept or implicitly reinforce the idea that corporate learning is only about learning functions 'doing something' to employees. They must find a way to bring businesses to bear.

THE TIPPING POINT

I believe that these five priorities are at the heart of what corporate learning functions need to do to create a tipping point. Yet I am aware that at least one question remains: what are we trying to create a tipping point towards, other than more effective corporate learning? What lies on the other side of it?

A clue can be found in learning leaders' reactions when I have presented my ideas to them. Generally speaking, they do not disagree. The jump from *learning* to *behaviour change* is bigger for some than for others, but as yet there have been no gasps of disbelief or outraged cries of denial. Indeed, what seems to concern them most is not the ideas themselves, but how to implement them. On the last two priorities, in particular, I have heard the occasional sharp intake of breath or long sigh, at the thought of strong impact evaluation or creating greater visibility around the business's role in the learning process.

There is a feeling, often unarticulated, that corporate learning's predicament, the crisis it finds itself in, is not all its own fault – that what is holding corporate learning back is not only corporate learning itself but also the broader business context. And here we find our profession in a reinforcing negative loop, a catch-22: learning functions are unsure of how to institute changes in the contexts in which they operate, yet at the same time the contexts won't change until learning functions do something to change them. And the more they don't change, the tougher the task of changing becomes.

This loop forms the very basis of our failure to improve corporate learning's satisfaction ratings. Bound by the ties of history and tradition, we go about the business of corporate learning in pretty much the same way as we did thirty years ago. Much has changed, of course, but fundamentally what we do is the same. But if we are to change the beliefs, attitudes and behaviours that businesses and their leaders have and demonstrate towards the activity of corporate learning, something has to break this loop, and it is up to us, as a profession, to make the first move.

What we are trying to create, what we are trying to tip towards, is a change in corporate learning's business context, which currently negatively impacts its ability to operate. The original learning organisation movement sought to optimise the business environment for the process of everyday learning. We are trying to optimise it for the effective functioning of corporate learning and learning functions. We are trying to create a context in which learning functions are viewed as a core and integral part of the strategic team, in which corporate learning is better understood as a complex and long-term task, and in which the task of learning is accepted as the responsibility of the whole business and not only the learning function. We are trying to create a new and rather different type of learning organisation: *Learning Organisation 2.0*. This does not mean that I do not support the ideas of the original learning organisation movement, it is just that I believe they will not come to fruition until businesses change how they think about and treat corporate learning and learning functions, and this will not happen until we as a profession start doing things differently.

This change is needed now more than ever because the development and deployment of learning solutions is becoming more challenging by the year. Organisations are increasingly expecting more for their learning money: moving to more cost-effective solutions, demanding faster design and delivery cycles and more accessible content. All of which places pressure on learning solutions by creating greater need for compromise in their development and deployment. The art of compromise – finding a way through what is best in theory and what is possible in practice – is a natural feature of all corporate learning. But I am concerned that the ability of learning functions to balance these different constraints is being undermined by the pressures of the modern business environment.

I stated at the beginning of this book that the reasons the original learning organisation concept faltered would act as new criteria for success: that we would need to find an environmentally embedded solution that makes sense in its time, that it would need to be practical and easily implementable, and that it would need to enable us to gain a better understanding of the ways our history channels our thinking so that we can adopt a more objective approach. I suggest that the five priorities I am advocating and the myriad smaller changes I have suggested amount to just this.

It is not the complete story, of course. These are just the first steps. Other issues will emerge as we go forward. Achieving a clearer and more detailed understanding of what organisations need to do to support corporate learning and learning functions still lies ahead of us. As does obtaining a clearer picture of how to go about changing behaviour and integrating methods and techniques from fields such as psychology, behavioural economics and psychotherapy. But these are stories for another day and, for the moment at least, taking these first steps will be challenge and victory enough.

References

1. Accenture (2004). *The Rise of the High-Performance Learning Organization: Results from the Accenture 2004 Survey of Learning Executives*. London: Accenture.

2. Accenture (2004). *The Rise of the High-Performance Learning Organization: Results from the Accenture 2004 Survey of Learning Executives*. London: Accenture.

3. Giangreco, A., Carugati, A. and Sebastiano, A. (2010). Are We Doing the Right Thing? Food for Thought on Training Evaluation and its Context. *Personnel Review*, 39(2), 162–177.

4. Accenture (2004). *The Rise of the High-Performance Learning Organization: Results from the Accenture 2004 Survey of Learning Executives*. London: Accenture.

5. Duke CE. (2009). *Learning and Development in 2011: A Focus on the Future*. Durham, NC: Duke Corporate Education.

6. Accenture (2004). *The Rise of the High-Performance Learning Organization*. London: Accenture.

7. CIPD (2011). *Learning & Talent Development Annual Survey Report*. London: CIPD.

8. Bersin, J. (2012). *The Corporate Learning Factbook*. Oakland, CA: Bersin & Associates.

9. Accenture (2004). *The Rise of the High-Performance Learning Organization: Results from the Accenture 2004 Survey of Learning Executives*. London: Accenture.

10. Straub, R. (1999). Knowledge Work in a Connected World: Is Workplace Learning the Next Big Thing? *Journal of Applied Research in Workplace E-learning*, 1(1), 5–11.

11. Collins, P. (2011, December). An Insider's View to Meeting the Challenges of Blended Learning Solutions. *Training & Development*, 65(12), 56–61.

12. Hofmann, J. and Miner, N. (2008, September). Real Blended Learning Stands Up. *Training & Development*, 62(9), 28–29.

13. Al-Hunaiyyan, A., Al-Huwail, N. and Al-Sharhan, S. (2008). Blended E-Learning Design: Discussion of Cultural Issues. *International Journal of Cyber Society and Education*, 1(1), 17–32.

14. Fleishman, E.A., Harris, E.F. and Burtt, H.E. (1955). *Leadership and Supervision in Industry: Monograph No. 33*. Columbus, OH: Personnel Research Board, Ohio State University.

15. Goldstein, I.L. (1980). Training in Work Organisations. *Annual Review of Psychology*, 31, 229–272.

16. Kessels, J. and Harrison, R. (1998). External Consistency: The Key to Success in Management Development Programmes? *Management Learning*, 29(1), 39–68.

17. Rouiller, J.Z. and Goldstein, I.L. (1993). The Relationship between Organisational Transfer Climate and Positive Transfer of Training. *Human Resource Development Quarterly*, 4(4), 377–390.

    Tracey, J.B., Tannenbaum, S.I. and Kavanagh, M.J. (1995). Applying Trained Skills on the Job: The Importance of the Work Environment. *Journal of Applied Psychology*, 80(2), 239–252.

18. Hirsh, W. (2005). *Developing and Delivering a Learning Strategy*. London: Corporate Research Forum.

19. CIPD (2011). *Learning & Talent Development Annual Survey Report*. London: CIPD.

20. Bersin, J. (2010). *The Business Value of Research in Corporate Learning and Human Resources*. Oakland, CA: Bersin & Associates.

21. McKinsey (2010). *Building Organizational Capabilities*. New York: McKinsey & Company.

    Human Capital Institute (2011). *Driving Performance and Business Results with Collaborative Executive Development*. New York: HCI.

22. Glenn, M. (2009, April). Making Sure the Solutions Are the Right Ones: Training Needs Analysis. *Training & Development in Australia*, 36(2), 18–21.

23. Barksdale, S. and Lund, T. (2001). *Rapid Needs Analysis: The ASTD Learning and Performance Workbook Series*. Alexandria, VA: ASTD.

24. ESI (2011). *Learning Trends Report*. London: ESI International.

25. Sitzmann, T., Kraiger, K., Stewart, D. and Wisher, R. (2006). The Comparative Effectiveness of Web-based and Classroom Instruction: A Meta-Analysis. *Personnel Psychology*, 59, 623–664.

26. Bonk, C.J. and Graham, C.R. (2006). *Handbook of Blended Learning: Global Perspectives, Local Designs*. San Francisco, CA: Pfeiffer Publishing.

27. Hirsh, W. (2005). *Developing and Delivering a Learning Strategy*. London: Corporate Research Forum.

28. Brennan, M. (2003). *Blended Learning and Business Change: Key Findings*. Framingham, MA: IDC.

29. Connell, M.W. (2012). *Designing Effective Learning Experiences with Learning Science*. Boston, MA: Native Brain, Inc.

30. Brewer, R. (2010, May). Finding Greatness in Training. *EHS Today*, 3(5), 40.

31. Kolb, D.A. (1984). *Experimental Learning*. Englewood Cliffs, NJ: Prentice Hall.

32. Honey, P. and Mumford, A. (1982). *The Manual of Learning Styles*. Maidenhead: Peter Honey.

33. Noe, R.A. (2003). *Employee Training and Development* (3rd edn). New York: McGraw-Hill.

34. Hirsh, W. (2005). *Developing and Delivering a Learning Strategy*. London: Corporate Research Forum.

35. Hirsh, W. (2005). *Developing and Delivering a Learning Strategy*. London: Corporate Research Forum.

36. Emelo, R. (2011, December). The Future of Learning. *Chief Learning Officer*, 18–21.

37. Overton, L. and Dixon, G. (2011). *Learning Technology Adoption in European Businesses*. Berlin: Online-Educa.

38. Duke Corporate Education (2009). *Learning and Development in 2011: A Focus on the Future*. Durham, NC: Duke Corporate Education.

39. Kamikow, N. (2011, November). Moving at Warp Speed. *Chief Learning Officer*, 4.

40. McKinsey (2010). *Building Organizational Capabilities*. New York: McKinsey & Company.

41. Hannon, J. and D'Netto, B. (2007). Cultural Diversity Online: Student Engagement with Learning Technologies. *International Journal of Educational Management*, 21(5), 418–432.

42. Sánchez, J., Salinas, A., Contreras, D. and Meyer, E. (2011). Does the New Digital Generation of Learners Exist? *British Journal of Educational Technology*, 42(4), 543–556.

43. CIPD (2008). *Gen Up: How the Four Generations Work*. London: CIPD.

44. CIPD (2008). *Who Learns at Work? Employees' Experiences of Workplace Learning*. London: CIPD.

45. Blain, J. (2011). *Training Today, Training Tomorrow: An Analysis of Learning Trends*. Bracknell: Cegos.

46. CIPD (2011). *Learning & Talent Development Annual Survey Report*. London: CIPD.

47. Duke CE. (2009). *Learning and Development in 2011: A Focus on the Future*. Durham, NC: Duke Corporate Education.

48. Blunt, R. (2007). Does Game-Based Learning Work? Results from Three Recent Studies. *The Interservice Industry Training Simulation Education Conference IITSEC*, 1, 945–954. NTSA.

49. Phillips, J., Phillips, P.P. and Zuniga, L. (2000). Evaluating the Effectiveness and the Return on Investment of E-learning. In M.E. Buren (ed.), *What Works Online: 2000, 2nd Quarter*. Alexandria, VA: American Society for Training and Development.

50. Salas, E., DeRouin, R. and Littrell, L. (2005). Research-Based Guidelines for Designing Distance Learning: What We Know So Far. In H.G. Gueutal, and D.L. Stone (eds), *The Brave New World of e-HR*, 104–137. San Francisco, CA: Jossey-Bass.

51. Flood, J. (2002). Read All About It: Online Learning Facing 80% Attrition Rates. *Turkish Online Journal of Distance Education*, 3(2), 79–84.

52. Rosman, P. (2008). M-learning – as a Paradigm of New Forms in Education. *E+M Ekonomie a Management*, 1, 119–125.

53. Wentworth, D. and Green, M. (2011, July). Mobile Learning: Anyplace, Anytime. *Training & Development*, 65(7), 25.

54. Kumar, L.S., Jamatia, B., Aggarwal, A.K. and Kannan, S. (2011). Mobile Device Intervention for Student Support Services in Distance Education. *European Journal of Open, Distance & E-Learning*, 2. Available at: www.eurodl.org/?article=447.

55. Buhagiar, A., Montebello, M. and Camilleri, V. (2010). Mobile Augmented Reality in an Arts Museum. *Proceedings of Mlearn2010: 10th World Conference on Mobile and Contextual Learning*, 395–397. Valetta: University of Malta.

56. Kearney, M., Schuck, S., Burden, K. and Aubusson, P. (2012). Viewing Mobile Learning from a Pedagogical Perspective. *Research in Learning Technology*, 20, 1–17.

57. Ebner, M. (2009). Introducing Live Microblogging: How Single Presentations Can Be Enhanced by the Mass. *Journal of Research in Innovative Teaching*, 2(1), 91–100.

58. Bartley, S.J. and Golek, J.H. (2004). Evaluating the Cost Effectiveness of Online and Face-to-Face Instruction. *Educational Technology & Society*, 7(4), 167–175.

59. Bersin, J. (2012). *The Corporate Learning Factbook*. Oakland, CA: Bersin & Associates.

60. Lohman, M.C. (2009). A Survey of Factors Influencing the Engagement of Information Technology Professionals in Informal Learning Activities. *Information Technology, Learning, and Performance Journal*, 25(1), 43–53.

61. Overton, L. and Dixon, G. (2011). *Learning Technology Adoption in European Businesses*. Berlin: Online-Educa.

62. Sitzmann, T. and Ely, K. (2011). A Meta-Analysis of Self-Regulated Learning in Work-Related Training and Educational Attainment: What We Know and Where We Need to Go. *Psychological Bulletin*, 137(3), 421–442.

63. Russell, T.L. (1999). *The No Significant Difference Phenomenon*. Raleigh, NC: North Carolina State University.

64. Blunt, R. (2007). Does Game-Based Learning Work? Results from Three Recent Studies. *The Interservice Industry Training Simulation Education Conference IITSEC*, 1, 945–954. NTSA.

65. Lohman, M.C. (2009). A Survey of Factors Influencing the Engagement of Information Technology Professionals in Informal Learning Activities. *Information Technology, Learning, and Performance Journal*, 25(1), 43–53.

66. Clark, R.E. (1983). Reconsidering Research on Learning from Media. *Review of Educational Research*, 53, 445–460.

67. Sitzmann, T., Kraiger, K., Stewart, D. and Wisher, R. (2006). The Comparative Effectiveness of Web-Based and Classroom Instruction: A Meta-Analysis. *Personnel Psychology*, 59, 623–664.

68. Hofmann, J. and Miner, N. (2008, September). Real Blended Learning Stands Up. *Training & Development*, 62(9), 28–29.

69. Al-Hunaiyyan, A., Al-Huwail, N. and Al-Sharhan, S. (2008). Blended E-Learning Design: Discussion of Cultural Issues. *International Journal of Cyber Society and Education*, 1(1), 17–32.

70. Hofmann, J. and Miner, N. (2008, September). Real Blended Learning Stands Up. *Training & Development*, 62(9), 28–29.

71. Hofmann, J. and Miner, N. (2008, September). Real Blended Learning Stands Up. *Training & Development*, 62(9), 28–29.

72. Lohman, M.C. (2009). A Survey of Factors Influencing the Engagement of Information Technology Professionals in Informal Learning Activities. *Information Technology, Learning, and Performance Journal*, 25(1), 43–53.

73. Chu, T.H. and Robey, D. (2008). Explaining Changes in Learning and Work Practice following the Adoption of Online Learning: A Human Agency Perspective. *European Journal of Information Systems*, 17, 79–98.

74. Lohman, M.C. (2009). A Survey of Factors Influencing the Engagement of Information Technology Professionals in Informal Learning Activities. *Information Technology, Learning, and Performance Journal*, 25(1), 43–53.

75. Verpoorten, D., Westera, W. and Specht, M. (2011). Using Reflection Triggers while Learning in an Online Course. *British Journal of Educational Technology*. Online version published before printed version, doi: 10.1111/j.1467–8535.2011.01257.x.

76. Bersin, J. (2012). *The Corporate Learning Factbook*. Oakland, CA: Bersin & Associates.

77. Corporate Leadership Council (2012). *Driving the Business Impact of L&D Staff*. London: The Corporate Executive Board Company.

78. Accenture (2004). *The Rise of the High-Performance Learning Organization: Results from the Accenture 2004 Survey of Learning Executives*. London: Accenture.

79. Accenture (2004). *The Rise of the High-Performance Learning Organization: Results from the Accenture 2004 Survey of Learning Executives*. London: Accenture.

80. Accenture (2004). *The Rise of the High-Performance Learning Organization: Results from the Accenture 2004 Survey of Learning Executives*. London: Accenture.

81. Corporate Leadership Council (2012). *Driving the Business Impact of L&D Staff*. London: The Corporate Executive Board Company.

82. McGurk, J. (2011). *Business Savvy: Giving HR the Edge*. London: Chartered Institute of Personnel and Development.

83. Lawler, E.E. and Mohrman, A.M. (2003). *Creating a Strategic Human Resource Organization: An Assessment of Trends and New Directions*. Stanford, CA: Stanford University Press.

84. Ulrich, D. (1999). *Delivering Results: A New Mandate for Human Resource Professionals*. Boston, MA: Harvard Business School Press.

85. Bersin, J. (2012). *The Corporate Learning Factbook*. Oakland, CA: Bersin & Associates.

86. Bersin, J. (2012). *The Corporate Learning Factbook*. Oakland, CA: Bersin & Associates.

87. Ulrich, D. and Eichinger, R. (1998). Delivering HR with an Attitude. *HR Magazine*, June, 155–161.

88. Corporate Leadership Council (2012). *Driving the Business Impact of L&D Staff*. London: The Corporate Executive Board Company.

89. Bersin, J. (2012). *The Corporate Learning Factbook*. Oakland, CA: Bersin & Associates.

90. Kopp, B., Matteucci, M.C. and Tomasetto, C. (2012, January). E-tutorial Support for Collaborative Online Learning: An Explorative Study on Experienced and Inexperienced E-tutors. *Computers & Education*, 58(1), 12–20.

91. Enlow, S. and Ertel, D. (2006, May/June). Achieving Outsourcing Success: Effective Relationship Management. *Compensation and Benefits Review*, 38, 50–55.

92. Chartered Institute of Personnel and Development (2009). *HR Outsourcing and the HR Function: Threat or Opportunity?* London: Chartered Institute of Personnel and Development.

93. Baldwin, T. and Danielson, C.C. (2000). Building a Learning Strategy at the Top: Interviews with Ten of America's CLOs. *Business Horizons*, 43(6), 5–14.

94. Sugrue, B. and Lynch, D. (2006, February). Profiling a New Breed of Learning Executive. *Training and Development*, 60(2), 51–56.

95. Sugrue, B. and DeViney, N. (2005). *Learning Outsourcing Research Report*. Alexandria, VA: American Society for Training & Development.

96. Accenture (2004). *The Rise of the High-Performance Learning Organization: Results from the Accenture 2004 Survey of Learning Executives*. London: Accenture.

97. Corporate Leadership Council (2012). *Driving the Business Impact of L&D Staff*. London: The Corporate Executive Board Company.

98. Sugrue, B. and DeViney, N. (2005) *Learning Outsourcing Research Report*. Alexandria, VA: American Society for Training & Development.

99. Galanaki, E. and Papalexandris, N. (2005). Outsourcing of Human Resource Management Services in Greece. *International Journal of Manpower*, 26(4), 382–396.

100. Greer, C.R., Youngblood, S.A. and Gray, D.A. (1999). Human Resource Management Outsourcing: The Make or Buy Decision. *The Academy of Management Perspectives*, 13(3), 85–96.

101. Anderson, C. (2009, September). Outsourcing Increase in 2010? *Chief Learning Officer*, 54–56.

102. Norman, T.J. (2009). *Outsourcing Human Resource Activities: Measuring the Hidden Costs and Benefits*. Minnesota: University of Minnesota.

103. Carter, A., Hirsh, W. and Aston, J. (2002). *Resourcing the Training and Development Function: Report 390*. Brighton, UK: Institute for Employment Studies.

104. Chartered Institute of Personnel and Development (2009). *HR Outsourcing and the HR Function. Threat or Opportunity?* London: Chartered Institute of Personnel and Development.

105. DeViney, N. and Sugrue, B. (2004). Learning Outsourcing a Reality Check. *Training & Development*, 58(12), 40–45.

106. Galanaki, E. and Papalexandris, N. (2005). Outsourcing of Human Resource Management Services in Greece. *International Journal of Manpower*, 26(4), 382–396.

107. Gainey, T.W., Klaas, B.S. and Moore, D. (2002). Outsourcing the Training Function: Results from the Field. *People and Strategy*, 25(1), 16–22.

108. Sugrue, B. and DeViney, N. (2005). *Learning Outsourcing Research Report.* Alexandria, VA: American Society for Training & Development.

109. Anderson, C. (2009, September). Outsourcing Increase in 2010? *Chief Learning Officer*, 54–56.

110. Trondsen, E. (2005, May). Offshore Outsourcing E-Learning Content. *E.learning Age*, 24–27.

111. Kern, T., Willcocks, L.P. and Van Heck, E. (2002). The Winner's Curse in IT Outsourcing: Strategies for Avoiding Relational Trauma. *California Management Review*, 44(2), 47–69.

112. Walther, B., Jrg, S. and Wolter, S.C. (2005). Shall I Train Your Apprentice? An Empirical Investigation of Outsourcing of Apprenticeship Training in Switzerland. *Education & Training*, 47(4/5), 251–269.

113. Gainey, T.W., Klaas, B.S. and Moore, D. (2002). Outsourcing the Training Function: Results from the Field. *People and Strategy*, 25(1), 16–22.

114. Society for Human Resource Management (2004). *Human Resource Outsourcing Survey Report.* Alexandria, VA: SHRM Research.

115. Enlow, S. and Ertel, D. (2006, May/June). Achieving Outsourcing Success: Effective Relationship Management. *Compensation and Benefits Review*, 38, 50–55.

116. Galanaki, E. and Papalexandris, N. (2005). Outsourcing of Human Resource Management Services in Greece. *International Journal of Manpower*, 26(4), 382–396.

117. Sugrue, B. and DeViney, N. (2005). *Learning Outsourcing Research Report.* Alexandria, VA: American Society for Training & Development.

118. Klaas, B.S., McClendon, J. and Gainey, T.W. (1999). HR Outsourcing and Its Impact: The Role of Transaction Costs. *Personnel Psychology*, 52(1), 113–136.

119. Enlow, S. and Ertel, D. (2006, May/June). Achieving Outsourcing Success: Effective Relationship Management. *Compensation and Benefits Review*, 38, 50–55.

120. Gainey, T.W., Klaas, B.S. and Moore, D. (2002). Outsourcing the Training Function: Results from the Field. *People and Strategy*, 25(1), 16–22.

121. Accenture (2004). *The Rise of the High-Performance Learning Organization: Results from the Accenture 2004 Survey of Learning Executives.* London: Accenture.

122. ESI (2011). *Learning Trends Report.* London: ESI International.

     CIPD (2011). *Learning & Talent Development Annual Survey Report.* London: CIPD.

123. Phillips, J.J. and Phillips, P.P. (2009, August). Measuring What Matters Most: How CEOs View Learning Success. *Training & Development,* 63(8), 44–49.

124. Campbell, J.P., Dunnette, M.D., Lawler, E.E. and Weick, K.E. (1970). *Managerial Behavior, Performance, and Effectiveness.* New York: McGraw-Hill.

125. Giangreco, A., Carugati, A. and Sebastiano, A. (2010). Are We Doing the Right Thing? Food for Thought on Training Evaluation and its Context. *Personnel Review,* 39(2), 162–77.

126. SHRM (2011). *The Ongoing Impact of the Recession – Recruiting and Skill Gap.* Alexandria, VA: SHRM.

127. Giangreco, A., Sebastiano, A. and Peccei, R. (2008). Trainees' Reactions to Training: An Analysis of the Factors Affecting Overall Satisfaction with Training. *The International Journal of Human Resources Management,* 20(1), 96–111.

     Iqbal, M.Z., Maharvi, M.W., Malik, S.A. and Khan, M.M. (2011). An Empirical Analysis of the Relationship between Characteristics and Formative Evaluation of Training. *International Business Research,* 4(1), 273–286.

128. Giangreco, A., Carugati, A. and Sebastiano, A. (2010). Are We Doing the Right Thing? Food for Thought on Training Evaluation and its Context. *Personnel Review,* 39(2), 162–77.

129. Pershing, J.A. and Pershing, J.L. (2001). Ineffective Reaction Evaluation. *Human Resources Development Quarterly,* 12(1), 73–90.

130. CIPD (2006). *Learning & Talent Development Annual Survey Report.* London: CIPD.

131. Sugrue, B. and Rivera, R.J. (2005). *State of the Industry: ASTD's Annual Review of Trends in Workplace Learning and Performance.* Alexandra, VA: ASTD.

132. Scriven, M. (1991). *Evaluation Thesaurus* (4th edn). Newbury Park, CA: Sage.

133. Rothwell, W.J. and Kazanas, H.C. (2008). *The Strategic Development of Talent* (2nd edn). Amherst, MA: HRD Press Inc.

134. Boverie, P., Mulcahy, D.S. and Zondlo, J.A. (1995). Evaluating the Effectiveness of Training Programs. In J.P. Pfeiffer (ed.), *The 1994 Annual: Developing Human Resources,* 279–294. San Diego, CA: Pfeiffer & Company.

135. Tannenbaum, S.I. and Woods, S.B. (1992). Determining a Strategy for Evaluating Training: Operating within Organizational Constraints. *Human Resources Planning,* 15(2), 63–81.

     Twitchell, S., Holton III, E.F. and Trott, J.R. (2001). Technical Training Evaluation Practices in the United States. *Performance Improvement Quarterly,* 13(3), 84–109.

136. Swanson, R.A. (2005). Evaluation, a State of Mind. *Advances in Developing Human Resources,* 7(1), 16–21.

137. Taylor, D.H. (2007, August). Why ROI on Training Doesn't Matter. *First Train*, 2(3), 18–19.

138. Spitzer, D.R. (1999). Embracing Evaluation. *Training*, 36(6), 42–47.

139. Salas, E. and Cannon-Bowers, J.A. (2001). The Science of Training: A Decade of Progress. *Annual Review of Psychology*, 52, 471–499.

140. Wang, G.G. and Wilcox, D. (2006, November). Training Evaluation: Knowing More than Is Practiced. *Advances in Developing Human Resources*, 8(4), 528–539.

141. Kraiger, K., McLinden, D. and Casper, W.J. (2004, Winter). Collaborative Planning for Training Impact. *Human Resource Management*, 43(4), 337–351.

142. Giangreco, A., Carugati, A. and Sebastiano, A. (2010). Are We Doing the Right Thing? Food for Thought on Training Evaluation and Its Context. *Personnel Review*, 39(2), 162–177.

143. ESI (2011). *Learning Trends Report*. London: ESI International.

144. Abernathy, D. (1999). Thinking Outside the Evaluation Box. *Training & Development*, 53(2), 19–23.

145. Wheeler, K. and Clegg, E. (2005). *The Corporate University Workbook*. San Diego, CA: Pfeiffer.

146. CIPD (2006). *Learning & Talent Development Annual Survey Report*. London: CIPD.

147. Kirkpatrick, D.L. (1959a). Techniques for Evaluating Training Programs: Part 1 – Reactions. *Journal of ASTD*, 13(11), 3–9.
Kirkpatrick, D.L. (1959b). Techniques for Evaluating Training Programs: Part 2 – Learning. *Journal of ASTD*, 13(12), 21–26.
Kirkpatrick, D.L. (1960a). Techniques for Evaluating Training Programs: Part 3 – Behavior. *Journal of ASTD*, 14(1), 13–18.
Kirkpatrick, D.L. (1960b). Techniques for Evaluating Training Programs: Part 4 – Results. *Journal of ASTD*, 14(12), 28–32.
Kirkpatrick, D.L. (1967). *Evaluation of Training*. New York: McGraw-Hill.

148. Giangreco, A., Carugati, A. and Sebastiano, A. (2010). Are We Doing the Right Thing? Food for Thought on Training Evaluation and Its Context. *Personnel Review*, 39(2), 162–177.

149. Alliger, G.M., Tannenbaum, S.I., Bennett, W., Traver, H. and Shotland, A. (1997). A Meta-Analysis of the Relations among Training Criteria. *Personnel Psychology*, 50, 341–358.

150. Holton, F.H. (1996). The Flawed Four-Level Evaluation Model. *Human Resources Development Quarterly*, 7(1), 5–20.

151. Wang, G.C., Dou, Z. and Li, N. (2002). A Systems Approach to Measuring Return on Investment for HRD Interventions. *Human Resource Development Quarterly*, 13(2), 203–224.

152. Bates, R. (2004). A Critical Analysis of Evaluation Practice: The Kirkpatrick Model and the Principle of Beneficence. *Evaluation and Program Planning*, 27(3), 341–348.

153. Tessmer, M. and Richey, R. (1997). The Role of Context in Learning and Instructional Design. *Educational Technology, Research and Development*, 45(3), 85–115.

154. Rouiller, J.Z. and Goldstein, I.L. (1993). The Relationship between Organisational Transfer Climate and Positive Transfer of Training. *Human Resource Development Quarterly*, 4(4), 377–390.

155. Warr, P., Bird, M. and Rackham, N. (1970). *Evaluation of Management Training: A Practical Framework, with Cases, for Evaluating Training Needs and Results*. London: Gower.

156. Worthen, B.R. and Sanders, J.R. (1987). *Educational Evaluation*. New York: Longman.

157. Bushnell, D.S. (1990). Input, Process, Output: A Model for Evaluating Training. *Training and Development*, 44(3), 41–43.

158. Alliger, G.M. and Janak, E.A. (1989). Kirkpatrick's Levels Of Training Criteria: 30 Years Later. *Personnel Psychology*, 42, 331–342.

159. Tan, J.A., Hall, R.J. and Boyce, C. (2003). The Role of Employee Reactions in Predicting Training. *Human Resource Development Quarterly*, 14(4), 397–411.
Rowold, J. (2007). Individual Influences on Knowledge Acquisition in a Call Center Training Context in Germany. *International Journal of Training and Development*, 11(1), 21–34.

160. Alliger, G.M. and Janak, E.A. (1989). Kirkpatrick's Levels of Training Criteria: 30 Years Later. *Personnel Psychology*, 42, 331–342.

161. Rouiller, J.Z. and Goldstein, I.L. (1993). The Relationship between Organisational Transfer Climate and Positive Transfer of Training. *Human Resource Development Quarterly*, 4(4), 377–390.
Antheil, J.H. and Casper, I.G. (1986). Comprehensive Evaluation Model: A Tool for the Evaluation of Non Traditional Educational Programs. *Innovative Higher Education*, 11(1), 55–64.

162. Alliger, G.M., Tannenbaum, S.I., Bennett, W., Traver, H. and Shotland, A. (1997). A Meta-Analysis of the Relations among Training Criteria. *Personnel Psychology*, 50, 341–358.

163. Dixon, N.M. (1987). Meet Training's Goals without Reaction Forms. *Personnel Journal*, 66(8), 108–115.

164. Iaffaldano, M.T. and Muchinsky, P.M. (1985). Job Satisfaction and Job Performance: A Meta-Analysis. *Psychological Bulletin*, 97, 251–273.

165. Phillips, J. (1996, April). Measuring ROI: The Fifth Level of Evaluation. *Technical & Skills Training*, 10–13.

166. ESI (2011). *Learning Trends Report*. London: ESI International.

167. Watkins, R., Leigh, D., Foshay, R. and Kaufman, R. (1998). Kirkpatrick Plus: Evaluation and Continuous Improvement with a Community Focus. *Educational Technology Research and Development*, 46(4), 90–96.

   Kaufman, R., Keller, J. and Watkins, R. (1995). What Works and What Doesn't: Evaluation beyond Kirkpatrick. *Performance & Instructions*, 35(2), 8–12.

168. Kraiger, K., McLinden, D. and Casper, W.J. (2004, Winter). Collaborative Planning for Training Impact. *Human Resource Management*, 43(4), 337–351.

169. McEvoy, G.M. and Buller, P.F. (1990). Five Uneasy Pieces in the Training Evaluation Puzzle. *Training & Development*, 44(8), 39–42.

   Boverie, P., Mulcahy, D.S. and Zondlo, J.A. (1995). Evaluating the Effectiveness of Training Programs. In J.P. Pfeiffer (ed.), *The 1994 Annual: Developing Human Resources*, 279–294. San Diego, CA: Pfeiffer & Company.

   Giangreco, A., Carugati, A. and Sebastiano, A. (2010). Are We Doing the Right Thing? Food for Thought on Training Evaluation and Its Context. *Personnel Review*, 39(2), 162–177.

170. Phillips, J.J. and Phillips, P.P. (2011, 6 August). The Myths of Return on Expectation. *Talent Management Magazine*.

171. Cascio, W.F. (1982). *Human Resources: The Financial Impact of Behavior in Organisations*. Boston, MA: Kent Publishing.

   Baldwin, T.T. and Ford, J.K. (1988). Transfer of Training: A Review and Directions for Future Research. *Personnel Psychology*, 41, 63–105.

172. Howard, G.S. and Dailey, P.R. (1979). Response-Shift Bias: A Source of Contamination of Self-Report Measures. *Journal of Applied Psychology Measures*, 64, 144–150.

   Conway, M. and Ross, M. (1984). Getting What You Want by Revising What You Had. *Journal of Personality and Social Psychology*, 47(4), 738–748.

173. Feltham, R. and Kinley, N. (2011, Summer). Strengths and Development Needs: Development of an Ipsative 360 Feedback Process as a New Approach to an Old Problem. *Assessment & Development Matters*, 3(2), 6–8.

174. Peterson, D.B. (1993). Measuring Change: A Psychometric Approach to Evaluating Individual Training Outcomes. Paper presented at the 8th annual conference of the Society for Industrial and Organizational Psychology. San Francisco, CA: SIOP.

175. Landsberger, H.A. (1958). *Hawthorne Revisited*. Ithaca, NY: Cornell University.

176. Dearden, L., Reed, H. and van Reenen, J. (2000). *Who Gains when Workers Train? Training and Corporate Productivity in a Panel of British Industries*. London: Institute for Fiscal Studies.

177. Michalski, G.V. and Cousins, J.B. (2001). Multiple Perspectives on Training Evaluations: Probing Stakeholder Perceptions in a Global Network Development Firm. *American Journal of Evaluation*, 22(1), 37–53.

178. Bean, R. (2009). *Winning in Your Own Way: The Nine and a Half Golden Rules of Branding*. London: Management Books 2000 Ltd.

179. Harris, P. (2008). It's Branding Time at the Learning Corral. *Training & Development*, 62(6), 41–45.

180. Cunningham, L. (2006). Branding of Learning and Development: Evidence from Research. *Development and Learning in Organizations*, 20(2), 7–9.

181. Papasolomou, I. and Vrontis, D. (2006). Building Corporate Branding through Internal Marketing: The Case of the UK Retail Bank Industry. *The Journal of Product and Brand Management*, 15(1), 37–47.

182. Expertus Inc. (2008). *Training Efficiency: Internal Marketing*. Santa Clara, CA: Expertus Inc.

183. Eccles, G. (2004). Marketing the Corporate University or Enterprise Academy. *Journal of Workplace Learning*, 16(7/8), 410–418.

184. Ettinger, A., Holton, V. and Blass, E. (2006). E-learner Experiences: A Lesson on In-House Branding. *Industrial and Commercial Training*, 38(1), 33–36.

185. Cunningham, L. (2006). Branding of Learning and Development: Evidence from Research. *Development and Learning in Organizations*, 20(2), 7–9.

186. Manning, P. (1991). Environmental Aesthetic Design: Identifying and Achieving Desired Environmental Effects, Particularly 'Image' and 'Atmosphere'. *Building and Environment*, 26(4), 331–340.

187. Appel-Meulenbroek, R., Havermans, D., Janssen, I. and van Kempen, A. (2010). Corporate Branding: An Exploration of the Influence of CRE. *Journal of Corporate Real Estate*, 12(1), 47–59.

188. Maister, D., Galford, R. and Green, C. (2000). *The Trusted Advisor*. London: Simon & Schuster.

189. Doyle, P. (1998). *Marketing Management and Strategy*. Hemel Hempstead: Prentice-Hall.

190. Appel-Meulenbroek, R., Havermans, D., Janssen, I. and van Kempen, A. (2010). Corporate Branding: An Exploration of the Influence of CRE. *Journal of Corporate Real Estate*, 12(1), 47–59.

191. Harris, P. (2008). It's Branding Time at the Learning Corral. *Training & Development*, 62(6), 41–45.

192. Ricketts, G. (2005, 1 March). Governance: The Next Learning Gap. *Chief Learning Officer Magazine*.

193. Bersin, J. (2008). *The High-Impact Learning Organization: What Works in the Management, Governance and Operations of Modern Corporate Training*. Oakland, CA: Bersin & Associates.

194. Bersin, J. (2008). *The High-Impact Learning Organization: What Works in the Management, Governance and Operations of Modern Corporate Training*. Oakland, CA: Bersin & Associates.

195. Mizruchi, M.S. and Stearns, L.B. (1988). A Longitudinal Study of the Formation of Interlocking Directorates. *Administrative Science Quarterly*, 33, 194–210.

196. Bersin, J. (2008). *The High-Impact Learning Organization: What Works in the Management, Governance and Operations of Modern Corporate Training.* Oakland, CA: Bersin & Associates.

197. Nanka-Bruce, D. (2011). Corporate Govemance Mechanisms and Firm Efficiency. *International Journal of Business and Management*, 6(5), 28–40.

198. Jensen, M. (1993). The Modem Industrial Revolution, Exit, and the Failure of Internal Control Systems. *Journal of Finance*, 48, 831–880.

199. Hambrick, D.C. and Fredrickson, J.W. (2001). Are You Sure You Have a Strategy? *Academy of of Management Executive*, 15, 48–59.

200. Charan, R. (2005). *Boards that Deliver.* San Francisco, CA: Jossey-Bass.

Index